CULTS

CULTS

IN TOO DEEP
FROM JONESTOWN
TO SCIENTOLOGY

LIGHTNING
GUIDES

FROM THE
EDITOR

"The only difference between a cult and a religion is the amount of real estate they own."

—FRANK ZAPPA

O n April 24, 2009, the two heiresses to the Seagram liquor fortune, Clare and Sara Bronfman, received an extortion letter. Signed by their beautician, financial planner, and masseuse, the letter demanded a payment of "$2.1 million by midnight," and threatened to blackmail the sisters if they did not promptly fulfill payment. Terrifying as this threat might have seemed, it would never have come to fruition.

The letter was fraudulent, and may have even been drawn up by, or with the knowledge of, the sisters themselves. The names on the extortion letter concealed the true recipients of the sisters' fortune—the cult organization NXIVM (pronounced "nexium"), which advertises itself as a multi-level marketing company offering personal and professional development classes. Both sisters had for years taken classes through NXIVM and even trained others.

Clare and Sara have never admitted (even under sworn testimony) that the extorted funds went directly to NXIVM, formerly known as Executive Success Programs. But they don't have to. Documents show that, over the course of a decade, Clare and Sara used over $150 million from their inheritance to fund NXIVM's real estate acquisitions and lawsuits, the purchase of a 22-seat Canadair CL-600 jet, and NXIVM founder Keith Raniere's failed investments. Clare and Sara may have transferred funds knowingly, but whether they did so of their own free will is completely up for question.

Many attribute the Bronfman sisters' attraction to NXIVM to their distant relationship with their father, Edgar Bronfman. Bronfman initially introduced the girls to the organization; he hoped NXIVM's self-improvement workshops would bring him closer to his daughters. Despite their wealth, Clare and Sara sought more, and believed they found it within NXIVM's group dynamic. Every day, people with admirable goals—to create familial bonds, to explore new identities, to contribute to society on a larger level—innocently join potentially dangerous social or religious organizations, unaware of the fact that they may be making their last sovereign choice, unaware that there may, in fact, be no way out.

CONTENTS

first, a few facts

In the 1960s, Charles Manson and the Manson Family lived in the LA mansion of Dennis Wilson, a member of the Beach Boys

There are over 2,000 cults in existence today

THE LEADER OF THE BRANCH DAVIDIANS WAS MURDERED BY ONE OF HIS OWN MEMBERS

20% of adults have participated in "new-religious" or "para-religious" movements

Jim Jones believed religion was the only force strong enough to produce a communist revolution

What is a cult?
Simply put, a cult is a group of people following an alternative belief system. However, a cult is far more complicated and better understood when considered as a process that happens over time. Initially, a charismatic individual assumes the role of the savior and attracts followers with a derivative, pseudo religious, or political doctrine. The term "cult" is usually applied when group activities become marked by participation in deviant sexual practices or violent acts against internal dissent or outside threats, real or perceived.

Why do people join cults?
The breakdown of established social orders, religious crisis, economic hardship, or political repression can all act as catalysts sending individuals in search of alternatives to failing social narratives. Cult initiates are usually vulnerable in some way, often struggling with money or relationships. However, just as often, new recruits can be entirely well-adjusted and still disillusioned with the status quo.

In what country are the majority of cults located?
Although a number of countries (including France and Germany) have banned cult-like activity, Western Europe and the United States have given rise to some of the most popular cults in recent history. New York and London were particularly fertile ground for Mormonism, Jehovah's Witnesses, and Crowleyism, while twentieth-century California reigned as the chosen home of sects like the Manson Family, Peoples Temple, Heaven's Gate.

Are all cults religious?

Most cults adopt previously perpetuated religious ideas, language, practices, or narrative elements but are not necessarily defined as religions. However, even the idea of religion is contestable. Scientology, critiqued by many, calls itself a religion; it is based on the belief that the ghosts of aliens that were massacred in an ancient, intergalactic, ethnic cleansing program inhabit the earth. Alternatively, billions of people accept the story of Christ's miracles, death, and resurrection at face value. Hence, the credibility of religious elements in cults seems to be based on the number of believers there are rather than in what they believe.

How does a mass suicide come about?

While the majority of cults do not end in mass suicide, instances like the Jonestown Massacre and Heaven's Gate have left a deep impression on peoples' understanding of cult practices. It is difficult to pinpoint a particular reason for this behavior. For cult members, mass suicides can be viewed as the pinnacle moment of societal rejection essential to most cults, as well as true salvation, only achieved from within the cult itself.

How is a cult different from a sect?

Though a sect can devolve into a cult, and both terms tend to carry a negative connotation, the two terms are not interchangeable. A sect is formed following a disagreement over doctrine in an established belief system. Often, sects are formed because of a power struggle within the organization. For example, when Christianity split between the Orthodox and Catholic churches, the Catholic denomination was seen as a "heresy" by its eastern counterpart. What sets a cult apart from a sect is the complete break from orthodoxy and an introduction of any number of taboo actions and rituals.

MASTERING MINDS

UNDERSTANDING CULT LEADERS

A happily-married wife and mother walks away from her husband and children with little notice. A bright teenager, captain of the cheer squad and honor roll student leaves her friends and family behind. Entire families, thousands at a time, uproot their lives (and often their life-savings) to follow the inane teachings and trajectories of a single soul. But, why? What is it that makes cults simultaneously formidable and irresistible? Most have had one thing in common: staunch leadership. Contemporary cults like Scientology, The Peoples Temple, Children of God, and Aleph (formerly known as Aum Shinrikyo), though varying in practice, are alike in that they each started out as a cult of one, led by and made up of an incredibly charismatic individual—an individual believing himself to be the spiritual guide without whom each cult would, inevitably, cease to be.

How do these men convince others to accept their messianic endeavors? Techniques vary. However, cult leaders often share

Left: Charles Manson set up a commune based on free love and devotion to himself. The Manson Family conducted a series of murders in California in 1969.

similar traits: diligence, commitment, assuredness, self-confidence, charisma, and intelligence. Likewise, so do most CEOs, entrepreneurs, and career activists. However, unlike other kinds of authoritative figures, cult leaders are often unable to separate their personal ideas from personal identities. In other words, the necessity to maintain control over employees, followers, family members, or other subordinates is imperative, as disagreeing with even a single belief or idea can be seen as a deliberate affront or rejection of the leader himself.

TRUSTING IN FALSE GODS

L. Ron Hubbard, Jim Jones, David Koresh, Marshall Applewhite, Charles Manson, David Berg, and Shoko Asahara—all leaders of some of the world's largest cults—have all been described by their followers using similar attributes: charismatic, confident, righteous, passionate, and driven. However, these men and other cult leaders do not selflessly embody these characteristics. Rather, they use them to cover fundamentally selfish personality traits, traits potentially destructive to anyone coming in contact with these individuals.

Not surprisingly, many cult leaders and their means of control are often classified under the Narcissistic Personality Disorder (NPD) profile. People with NPD tend to have an inflated sense of self-importance, lack empathy, and have a deep need for admiration from others. Often, these traits cover a fragile self-esteem that is sensitive to even the slightest criticism.

The American Psychiatric Association associates NPD with the following criteria:

- Having an exaggerated sense of self-importance
- Exaggerating achievements and talents

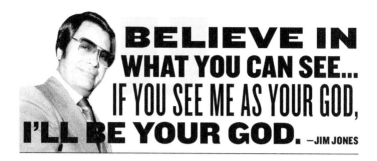

BELIEVE IN WHAT YOU CAN SEE... IF YOU SEE ME AS YOUR GOD, I'LL BE YOUR GOD. —JIM JONES

- Expecting to be recognized as superior without achievements that warrant it
- Being preoccupied with fantasies about success, power, brilliance, beauty, or the perfect mate
- Believing that you are superior and can only be understood by or associate with equally special people
- Requiring constant admiration
- Having a sense of entitlement
- Expecting special favors and unquestioning compliance with your expectations
- Taking advantage of others to get what you want
- Having an inability or unwillingness to recognize the needs and feelings of others
- Being envious of others and believing others envy you
- Behaving in an arrogant or haughty manner

The relationship dynamics in cults reflect most of the above traits. Leaders often make outlandish claims of being able to save lost and tortured souls or knowing how, when, and why the world will end. They ask followers to subscribe to a lifestyle that often includes giving up material belongings, money, independent thinking, and relationships outside of the cult. Cults led by men, as

many are, almost always impose excessive or prohibitive sexual requirements on women members as a condition of remaining a part of the group. These sacrifices are packaged as part of a gospel or teaching that only the leader can truly understand. As such, the laws of each cult's religious or social doctrine are subject to change at the leader's will, leaving members completely vulnerable to and reliant upon their leader's guidance.

If the cult guides a member's entire life, without clear and direct leadership, the member can easily feel unmoored, susceptible to outside influence.

Cults, functioning as intended, direct members' lives, with daily cult activities and rituals serving as the only guideposts of reality and accountability. Without clear and direct leadership, any member could easily feel unmoored and susceptible to outside influence. Leaders understand this and do all in their power to avoid losing their spot as central figure in their members' lives. Those members unwilling to conform to cult requirements are often excommunicated, subjected to intense

Right: Image from brochure of the Peoples Temple portraying cult leader Jim Jones as the loving father of the "Rainbow Family."

peer pressure, or, as alleged in Scientology, denied food, water, human contact, and held against their will until they comply.

Scientists are still researching the causes of NPD and do not make claims to fully understand its origins. Some research points to genetic factors while other studies examine home life and community influences. Even without a full understanding of the psychological factors contributing to the development of a cult leader, a historical perspective suggests that the late 1960s through the 1970s contained powerful social forces providing fertile soil for a host of narcissistic self-proclaimed messiahs.

DECADES OF DEVIANCE

In the decades following World War II, the United States experienced massive social change transforming nearly every part of society. The Baby Boomer generation (born between 1946 and 1964) challenged every traditional institution in American society from political parties to religious organizations. Driving this agitation, among many other catalysts, was a deep discontent with a status quo that sent tens of thousands to die in the Vietnam War, and treated African American people as second-class citizens. Replacing the traditional loci of society was a new narrative that melded political philosophy, new age spiritualism, and consumer desire while placing the individual at the center of everything. The desire was to stand out rather than fit in. Authoritative figures capitalized off of this shift.

Founded by Werner H. Erhard, Erhard Seminars Training (EST) was just one of many organizations that promoted alternative modes of existence during the 1970s. EST originally offered "The EST Standard Training" (a 60-hour course involving Socratic interrogation; sessions lasted from 9 a.m. to 12 a.m. with only one food break) encouraging participants to be truer versions of themselves rather than take on the roles society had forced upon them. Like many philosophical theories from the period, EST was purposefully nebulous; suggesting that participants were allowed to find their own meaning during the training sessions. EST's standard training was called "the technology of transformation," and focused on the value of integrity—an integrity that included not wearing watches, not speaking until spoken to, and recognizing that most of each participant's personal misery came as a function of their own broken agreements. In contrast, participants were also told that they were perfect as they were, but then questioned (often antagonistically) about whether they fully understood this idea.

EST leaders, through their techniques of personal transformation, reoriented members' expressions of identity from securely located within their communities to standing apart as an individual connected to, but not defined by, their communities. Ironically, in convincing participants that EST leaders could facilitate the transformation to a higher state of individualism, they also convinced participants to both willfully endure and pay for psychological and physical pressures that could potentially lead to death—as suggested in the case of Jack Andrew Slee, a bank teller who went to EST for help with nervous interactions with strangers, and died during "the danger process" involved in a 16-hour training. Of course, EST was not the only organization whose leaders were successful in manipulating minds to their will during this time.

Although many have found fault with EST, thousands have claimed that the organization (like a number of groups associated with the Human Potential Movement) helped them achieve higher levels of self-esteem and what Abraham Maslow termed self-actualization. For Maslow and followers of the Human Potential Movement, self-actualization meant not only understanding one's full potential, but reaching it. For, "What a man can be, he must be," Maslow once proclaimed.

Disillusioned by the dominant social structure, many people in the 1960s and 1970s sought to find or create alternative belief systems that explained both why society had failed and what could be done with that failure. It was a time of deep questioning without clear answers. Some individuals stepped up to provide answers and serve as a savior for those in need of guidance. Needless to say, Jim Jones, L. Ron Hubbard, David Berg, Father Yod, and other cult leaders did so with disappointing, if not deadly, results.

VACUOUS VISION

The Curious Claims of Convincing Leaders

JOSEPH SMITH

The founder of the Mormon Church was compelled to start his religion after being visited by an angel who directed him to a cache of buried rune-covered golden plates. After looking into a hat containing a "seer stone," Smith was able to translate the plates into The Book of Mormon.

SUN MYUNG MOON

On Easter morning 1935, Jesus appeared before the founder of the Unification Church and, according to Moon, anointed him to finish Christ's work by becoming father to all humanity.

MARSHALL APPLEWHITE

In 1972 the co-founder of the Heaven's Gate doomsday cult had a near-death experience brought on by a heart attack. The hallucination during this experience convinced him that the same extraterrestrial spirit that had previously guided Jesus inhabited him.

WHEN MEN WERE GODS

CONTEMPORARY CULTS WERE NOT THE FIRST TO WORSHIP MEN

Roman Emperor Diocletian adopted an ancient Persian belief that rulers were descendants of gods. He applied this belief to Roman political structure. Diocletian faith spawned cults that worshipped the emperor as divinity. The origin of many European monarchical claims of divine blood can be traced back to Diocletian.

Ancient Greek mystery cults were a common practice. Official state religions coexisted with many derivative or precursor beliefs. Individuals could participate in as many mysteries—secret rites, ceremonies and practices—as they wanted as long as these mysteries weren't publicly discussed.

Roman death cults were not as sinister as they sound. Following Diocletian's edict that emperors descended from gods, people began worshiping fallen Roman rulers. As such, the death mask of deceased emperors served as the cults' idols. In fact, not belonging to a death cult could be considered disrespectful to the state.

Worship of a single god was not unheard of before Christianity. Hypsistarians, a Mediterranean sect active from 200 BC to AD 400, devoted their faith to a concept loosely translated from Hellenic to Hebrew as "highest."

Religious ritual, divine vision, and cultic rites have long been associated with psychedelics, or hallucinogens. The drugs were likely components of the Eleusinian Mysteries (right), popular ceremonies in the ancient world celebrating the agrarian cycle of sowing and reaping. Persephone's yearly trip to the underworld was a major component of this mystery.

Egyptian goddess, Isis, was believed to be the mother of the Pharaoh and was often depicted as the throne in Egyptian symbology. As with many female goddesses, Isis was associated with fertility: the cyclical flooding of the Nile was ascribed to the tears of Isis as she wept for her son Osiris.

Apotheosis, the transformation of a man to a god, was conferred upon Alexander the Great after he integrated rituals from his many subjugated kingdoms into his court. Alexander's likeness was used for the reproduction of many gods (including Zeus and Pan) and in currency and statues throughout his empire.

ORDINARY
PEOPLE

FINDING AND LOSING THE SELF

Though there are common conditions that can create a social environment ripe for cults, there are no traits that necessarily create, for certain, a cult follower. As evidenced in the opening story of the Bronfman sisters, everyday people—young or old, rich or poor, educated and uneducated—seek connection, discipline, and acceptance through cult activities. In fact, the commonly held idea that someone joins a cult because they are ignorant or uneducated is a myth. It may well be that the opposite is true, that the intellectually curious and educated individual is most at risk of joining a cult. Why? Because no one joins a cult. People do, however, join reformed religious institutions, progressive political parties, spiritual centers, self-help groups, community associations or other surrogate social organizations seeking to change their lives or the lives of others.

A REASONABLE PROPOSITION

One of the most common ways cults attract members is by appealing to an inherent desire to do something good. A large number of cult members enter because they have the desire to experience something better (without knowing what that "better" might be) or be a part of a body of people positively contributing to the world in which they live. Just as most cult intakes join out of a desire to do good, most members recruit others because they're most often made to believe that their actions are necessary to enhance the life of another, particularly other cult members. Understandably so, the desire to engage and improve could be a powerful draw for almost anyone.

Just imagine, you aren't in a hurry, and an attractive, charismatic person politely approaches you to see if you're interested in taking a survey, one that will be used to improve the social conditions of your hometown. Throughout the process, the person interviewing you is very attentive (even intuitive) to your answers and reacts positively to all suggestions that you make. You feel (as many former cult members have reportedly felt) that you are really being listened to, perhaps for the first time in your life; your ideas and suggestions are truly being acknowledged. At the end of the

survey, your interviewer explains that he or she believes you have excellent insights and invites you to a community organization meeting to share them. Whether you know it or not, you have just been invited to your initial introduction to the cult.

If the preceding sounds believable, it's because it's real. This tactic is used every day to lure unassuming individuals into cult activities and associations. For instance, PSI Mind Development Institution, a California-based organization believed to be a cult (or, according to PSI.com, "the oldest continuously-operating personal and professional training company in the U.S.," specializing in large-group awareness training), uses this technique to to attract more than half a million people to its seminars. Other cults have appealed to more base instincts when attracting membership.

HOOKERS FOR JESUS

Children of God (COG), also known as The Family, is a California-based cult that used selective Bible passages to create a devious membership recruitment program. Adapting

> **Jesus Babies** The name given to children who were conceived from The Family's flirty fishing practice

scripture to the free love ethos of the early 1970s, founder David Berg interpreted "God is love" in a novel and audacious way. Finding inspiration in Matthew 4:19 when Jesus says, "Follow me and I will make you fishers of men," Berg proposed a strategy for his female followers: trade sex for money for the church and use sex to get more members. He called his idea "flirty fishing" and cryptically discussed it in a COG newsletter:

Q:"What is FF'ing?" Many of you asked for a definition and what should be reported as actual FF'ing.

A: We would like to answer that FF'ing is going out witnessing the love of Jesus with the serious intent to use sex or sex appeal as the bait, regardless of the situation or place. This can be anywhere!—On the street, in a park, while going to the local store, in discotheques or in clubs!

Q: Does "Loved Sexually" also include kissing and light petting?

A: We suggest you only include masturbation, sucking and actual intercourse in the figures of fish, mate, brother or sister loved sexually. It's all, or nothing at all! Hallelujah!

Difficult as it may be to believe, Berg's followers adopted the strategy with gusto and, according to internal COG documents, more than 220,000 "fish" were loved.

Flirty Fishing died out in the 1980s with developing concerns about AIDS. However, COG still practices "love bombing," when a group of people surround a member or potential recruit and give them intense amounts of affection and attention. Margaret Singer (a psychiatrist who testified on behalf of the British newspaper *The Daily Mail* during a libel trial involving COG) claimed that love bombing was a more effective brainwashing technique than the known means by which North Koreans suppressed prisoners of war.

POSITIVE FEEDBACK

Though the techniques used can be suspicious, cult indoctrination is usually based on positive action and ideology. New members are introduced to a social group that is self-assured of its own aims, mutually supportive, and, most importantly, inclusive. For instance, the membership of the Branch Davidians of Waco, Texas was racially integrated and women were in the majority. Indeed, part of what makes cults so difficult to reject is that their memberships and belief systems often appear to be representative of equality, respect, and trust, all attractive ideas to people aiming to escape the struggles of everyday society.

Former cult members often describe the early days of their experience nearly universally. Their experiences usually included a strong sense of belonging, a focus on important world issues, and activities driven by purpose, producing undeniably tangible results. Members subscribe to a simplified worldview directed by day-to-day cult life and supported by cult teachings and workshops. For many, the security provided by cult discipline, particularly as it relates to imparted knowledge and skill, is enough to convince that they need the cult more than they need the fear or confusion related to the outside world.

If a meaningful life is the promise of joining a cult, dependency is the life-blood that sustains them. The strength of this dependency

Large-group awareness training refers to activities offered by groups linked with the human potential movement. Erupting from the counterculture milieu of the 1960s and 1970s, the human potential movement advocates for an exceptional quality of life and claims to increase self-awareness, catalyzing desirable transformations in participants', personal lives.

is in part because almost every member brings and represents assets (usually benefiting the leader), be they monetary, organizational, structural (many members are recruited to cults in order to have their homes used as operating stations for specific cult branches) or otherwise. Leaders and loyal members will go to great lengths to avoid attrition for, because expected member dissent also introduces the risk of being discovered by authorities. Additionally, former followers may share the secrets of the cult. More damaging than any of these losses, however, is the possibility that other members of the cult may also consider leaving. One of the most important parts of cult membership retention, despite the many cults that draw new members by convincing them of their unrealized individualism, is the maintenance of empathy and connection among all cult members. This connection must also be understood as an extension of the cult leader so that everyone is accountable to each other first, and the leader ultimately.

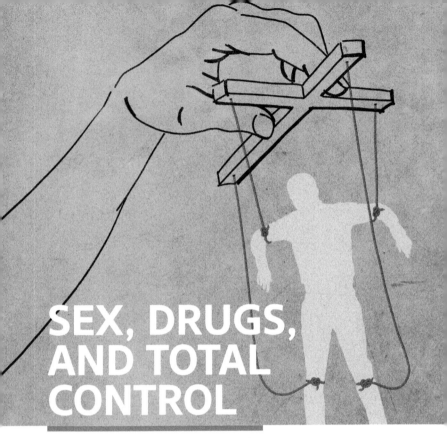

SEX, DRUGS, AND TOTAL CONTROL

THE MEANS TO MASS MALLEABILITY

Every cult needs followers for survival. Using drugs, sex, and systematic psychological and physiological manipulation, cults have perfected ways of ensuring that any attempt to leave is a painful, alienating, and sometimes deadly process.

GETTING ATTACHED

Membership retention begins with work, and a lot of it. As a means of bonding through labor, cult members are often tasked with insurmountable duties such as (in the case of Jim Jones' Peoples Temple) caring for San Francisco's entire homeless population. While there may exist a logical reason for cult's requiring members to commit so much time to any given cause (the future of the world is at stake, for instance) there's also a more sinister reason—isolation. Cults need followers to be dependent on the cult for everything from their material needs to their emotional well-being. The most sure way to create that dependence is by cutting away members' personal, professional, and family ties. Relationships take time. Cult accountability succeeds in monopolizing that time, ensuring that all outside bonds fall away.

Counterintuitively, former cult members have stated that the lack of outside involvement and freedom was a kind of freedom itself. In place of too many options and responsibilities, and more information than one individual can feasibly process, the singular duty of the cult can be extremely attractive.

UNDENIABLE IMPACT

Whether religious or self-help centered, cults understand that people looking for life changes are also seeking information. Cults allocate huge amounts of resources to not only providing this information, but also ensuring that the information provided reassures members of their necessary and undeniable purpose within the cult.

- The Children of God, founded by David Berg in 1968, published more than 20 independent periodicals recruiting members and explaining core doctrine. The group soon

expanded into new forms of media and even developed bespoke software programs that followers could use to securely access church information.

- Scientology, founded by L. Ron Hubbard, famously began as a book, *Dianetics*. Hubbard understood the importance that PR would play in building his church and created a film and publishing division specific to creating media that would attract followers.

Controlling exposure to outside media is one of the most important component of retaining cult members. For this reason, many cults, from Heaven's Gate to Scientology, produce their own literature while preaching a simpler, less technologically encumbered lifestyle. Removing television, books, periodicals, radio, and the Internet from followers' lives not only ensures that followers do not encounter critical commentary, but also ensures they will not be exposed to concepts that challenge the cult's belief system.

SACRED PROSTITUTION

Sexuality and identity are fundamentally entwined. Cult leaders seem to know and understand that breaking down a person's

February 2, 1971, members of Children of God sing before sitting down for lunch at their headquarters building in the Skid Row section of Los Angeles.

control over their own body is a powerful way to create a compliant follower. As such, sex, as a tool of domination and manipulation, is a recurrent phenomenon within cults. Once the individual relinquishes self-control, he or she is fully subservient, perfectly devoted to the cult leader. Cult leaders also use sexual control to minimize familial interconnectedness—between parent and child, husband and wife—and reorient attention and attachment to themselves.

Dwight York of the United Nuwaubian Nation of Moors, dictated how, when, and with whom his members had sex while helping himself to hundreds of young boys and girls, offering them entrance to heaven in exchange for forced molestation. Jim Jones exposed himself to and raped his male followers, often in front of the congregation—this was intended to prove that he was indeed "the only true heterosexual." David Koresh annulled all marriages between members of the Branch Davidians, giving himself exclusive right to sleep with anyone he chose, male or female. Charles Manson required his following (which was majority female) to submit to sex on demand as a condition of membership. David Berg turned all female members of The Family International into prostitutes; he also claimed incest and child molestation as a tenet of the cult's doctrine. This list could and does, unfortunately, continue. Although most cult leaders' rules concerning sex stem entirely from personal preference, few are above creating cult guidelines or citing and bastardizing accepted religious verses to back up their beliefs.

GETTING HIGH ON JESUS

Drugs have long been associated with cult rituals; however, drug use is not (as many assume) necessarily a cornerstone of all cult philosophy. For instance, the Manson Family spoke very publically about using LSD, but, again, LSD did not serve as a central factor in Charles Manson's visions of race war or in his many theological ramblings. Aleister Crowley wrote often of his recreational drug use, but drug use does not serve a prominent function in Crowley's religious philosophy, Thelema.

Have illicit drugs played a significant role in cults? Yes. As early as the 16th century, Spanish missionaries used a hallucinogen identified as ololiuqui (derived from the seeds of the morning glory). In pre-Colonial America, drugs were often utilized in religious rituals; Native American churches still continue the use of peyote and mescaline (hallucinogens derived from the cactus *Lophophora williamsii*) in ancient prayer ceremonies to this day. However, drug

ACQUIESCENCE

A Visual Exploration of Mass Cult Murder and Suicide

30+ 👤

HEAVEN'S GATE, 1997

Cause of Death: Phenobarbital mixed with applesauce served with a vodka chaser followed by asphyxiation from plastic bags wrapped around the head.

50+ 👤

ORDER OF THE SOLAR TEMPLE, 1994

Cause of Death: Multiple murderous ceremonies consisting of poison, smothering, and bullets to the head.

700+ 👤👤👤👤👤👤👤👤👤👤👤👤👤👤👤👤

MOVEMENT FOR THE RESTORATION OF THE TEN COMMANDMENTS OF GOD, 2000

Cause of Death: Mass murder by poison, strangulation, fire, explosives, and stabbing over the course of several weeks and in multiple locations.

900+ 👤👤👤👤👤👤👤👤👤👤👤👤👤👤👤👤👤👤

JONESTOWN MASSACRE, 1978

Cause of Death: Grape Flavor Aid mixed with cyanide, Phenergan, Valium, and chloral hydrate.

'Anonymous' protest at Church of Scientology, London. Man holds poster about the death of Lisa McPherson (February 10, 1959 – December 5, 1995).

use in contemporary cults, particularly in the 1960s and 1970s, is somewhat paradoxical. Stemming from the popularization of nicotine, narcotics, and alcohol during the youth movement and growing interest in the cultic and occult, contemporary cult drug use was most often isolated within the habits of the cult leader. Additionally, rather than encouraging the use of hallucinogens to reach transcendental levels promised to cult members, narcotics, when used on members, were a means of mass control and manipulation.

ONE OF US

By far the most effective way cults prohibit members' withdrawal is through peer pressure. Followers are forbidden from talking to those who leave—and those who disobey are punished. The decision to leave must be made in secrecy as members are trained to report anyone who discusses it. If discovered, the person looking to escape will likely be questioned by the cult leader and those closest to him or her will employ guilt, disappointment, and revulsion as a way to get them to stay. Some cults go to further lengths, using "reorientation" techniques to get members to stay.

Anyone never having been in a cult might have a hard time comprehending the power that cults have over their members. Consider Lisa McPherson, a Scientologist who died in 1995. McPherson was in a car accident but unharmed. Paramedics initially released her from the scene but later took her to a hospital after she began removing her clothes; she reported saying that she thought if she undressed she would receive counseling. While under observation at a Clearwater, Florida hospital a group of fellow Scientologists visited her and shortly thereafter she asked to be released. (Scientology is adamantly opposed to psychology and it is likely that the church did not want McPherson to undergo treatment.) McPherson was put on what Scientologists call an "isolation watch," which consisted of being left alone in a room. She died a few days later of dehydration and a coroner's report noted that she had not had water for more than 5 days. Her family claimed she was being held against her will.

The dynamics at play in recruiting and retaining cult members are a complex interplay of dissatisfaction with the status quo, ego, subservience, group identity, and exploitation. While many write off cult members as having joined of their own free will and think that they can leave at any time, in reality, leaving a cult requires a personal strength that few people possess.

DEVOLUTION

BAPTIST BELIEFS LED
TO BRANCH DAVIDIANS

David Koresh, the self-proclaimed reincarnation of Jesus and spiritual leader of the Branch Davidians, inherited a theology that traces its roots back to upstate New York's "burnt district," a tract of land so heavily envangelized in the mid-1800s that a biographer noted that there was no more "fuel" (converts) to "burn" (convert).

William Miller, a lay preacher for the Baptist church, believed he knew when the Second Advent of Jesus Christ would happen. He published a book outlining his research to popular appeal in 1834. The theology behind it became known as Millerism. Following Christ's failure to appear, followers of Millerism sectionalized and created their own interpretations, one of whom was Ellen G. White. White's writings would form much of the ideology behind the Seventh Day Adventist Church, formally established in 1863.

Victor Houteff, a Hungarian immigrant, led a reformist movement within the Seventh Day Adventist Church in the 1930s. His interpretation of scripture would lead to the formation of Davidian Seventh-day Adventist church. When Houteff died in 1955, Davidian Seventh-day Adventist member Benjamin Roden began exposing his own version of scripture, which he named Branch Davidianism. The Branch Davidians formalized their belief the same year Houteff died, 1955. David Koresh assumed leadership in 1989.

In little more than 150 years, Baptist theology, which traces it own roots to Protestantism, underwent three revisionist evolutions to become a cult located in Waco, Texas. The differences between the iterations come down to personal interpretation over theological details, failed predictions, or power struggles. What ties them all together is the changing nature of their followers; dissatisfied with existing doctrine, members set out to create new faiths in their own image.

Left: 1998, Branch Davidian leader, David Koresh, in a police line-up following a gun battle with former Davidians.

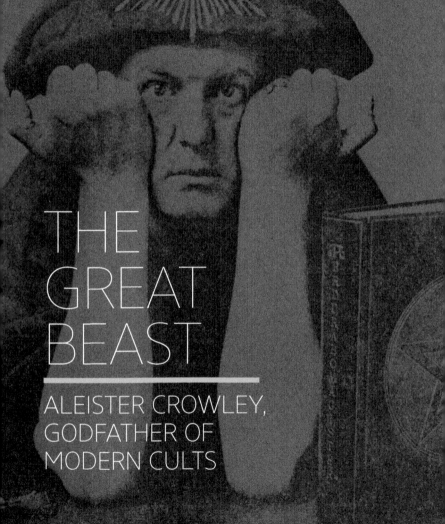

THE
GREAT
BEAST

ALEISTER CROWLEY,
GODFATHER OF
MODERN CULTS

Deciphering Aleister Crowley's (born Edward Alexander Crowley in England, 1875) life is no easy task. This is in part because Crowley spent a large portion of his time working for the British government as a spy. Though the Home Office (a ministerial department of the Government of the United Kingdom) has never officially acknowledged his role, several historians have all but sealed the case in his favor. Crowley, an accomplished mountain climber, poet, and occult hero, is a remarkably complex person.

His life's work, however, was Thelema, a religious lifestyle guide he founded on the teachings of earlier mystic traditions. Thelema exerted a profound influence on cults and alternative belief systems that sprang up during the cultural revolution of the 1960s and beyond.

PARADOXICAL REACTION

Crowley was born into a affluent family who practiced an obscure form of fundamentalist Christianity. Crowley was raised by his mother, who nicknamed him "The Beast". His father died when he was 11, leaving Crowley a third of his estate. From his early days, Crowley showed promise as a student but continually butted up against authoratative figures. One such figure was the headmaster of Cambridge preparatory school, Reverend Henry d'Arcy Champney, whom Crowley considered a sadist.

While at Cambridge, Crowley was introduced to the British tradition of private orders. Part social club, part learning salon, such orders are interested in revisiting esoteric pastimes. Crowley joined the Hermetic Order of the Golden Dawn, which focused on self-improvement and magical practices including scrying and ciphering; W. B Yeats,

Left: British occultist, writer, philosopher, and mystic Aleister Crowley

Florence Farr, and Evelyn Underhill were also members. Some Crowley biographers think that it was during this time that the British Intelligence agency approached him about spying. He studied philosophy and literature at Cambridge but dropped out in 1898 at the age of 23.

Shortly after leaving Cambridge Crowley began travelling extensively, a passion funded by his large inheritance and also serving as a cover for his government work. Crowley immersed himself in the native mystic traditions of Mexico and the teaching of Buddhism and Hinduism in India. Throughout this travels, he climbed mountains and composed a great deal of poetry, eventually marrying Rose Edith Kelly in 1903. Their honeymoon in Paris and Cairo would sow the first of the seeds that later blossomed into Thelema.

A VOICE NOT MY OWN

While in Cairo in 1904, Crowley and Kelly closely studied the religious beliefs of Ancient Egypt. One day Crowley heard a voice in his head, calling his name; he understood it to be Aiwass, the messenger of the Egyptian God Horus. Over the next three days Crowley transcribed everything Aiwass told him, calling the result *The Book of the Law*. It would become the founding text of Thelema.

Unsure of what to do with *The Book of the Law*, Crowley sent the manuscript to several acquaintances and then largely forgot about it. While he supposedly received other visitations from Aiwass and penned more books resulting from them over the next few years, it was not until 1909 that Crowley finally revisited the original tome and began to devote his life to practicing what the voice inside him had preached.

Thelema draws chiefly from the mystic traditions of the world's established religions and wrapped these influences in the rituals of the more recent European occult movements Crowley studied as a member of Hermetic Order of the Golden Dawn. Thelema's guiding belief: "Do what thou wilt shall be the whole of the Law. Love is the law, love under will." Later detractors of Crowley often selectively edited the phrase to say, "Do what though wilt," and labeled it a dressed up form of hedonism, which Crowley's lifestyle did nothing to disabuse. While this was part of what Crowley meant, the phrase, and Thelema itself, also had a deeper and more nuanced meaning. In encouraging his disciples to follow their "True Will," Crowley meant perfectly aligning one's lifestyle with the deepest impulses of one's spiritual nature and annihilating the self as it merged with the universe.

Ideologically, Thelema may be a positivist attempt at humanism, however, Crowley, being a recalcitrant contrarian, often made Thelema seem much more controversial through his actions. Crowley was prone to fits of passion and could often be cruel, especially to those close to him. He regarded women as morally and intellectually inferior to men. Publically bisexual, Crowley published several volumes of homoerotic poetry, in a time that punished such behavior with jail and hard labor. He was also a racist, considering all non-white races to be inferior. Many critics conclude that Crowley hadn't left the racial and social prejudices of his upper-class upbringing as far behind as he would like to believe.

Thelema was likewise vilified for its incorporation of sex magic rituals and occasional usage of animal blood or human feces. Opportunistic critics often chose Crowleyisms out of context. Quoted in the British tabloids, Crowley said, "A male child of perfect innocence and high intelligence is the most satisfactory victim". The tabloid said that it referred to human sacrifice but it was actually about Crowley's thoughts on masturbation. Despite the fact that they were untrue, Crowley often embraced such rumors and reveled in the title bestowed upon him by a conservative British tabloid of the times as "the wickedest man in the world."

THE CULT THAT NEVER WAS

Thelema has had a large influence on alternative belief systems that followed in its wake. However, during his own lifetime Crowley could not establish a flourishing cult. This is likely because of Crowley's refusal to be seen as a god. He repeatedly stated to followers of Thelema that the religion was more important than its messenger. Followers were free to leave whenever they wanted. And Crowley, himself, was never in one place long enough to establish a physical base or following. Unlike other cult leaders that committed themselves solely to their beliefs, Crowley spent much of his time painting, composing verse, and writing. He did not believe in Christian theology; Thelema draws on a body of knowledge so far from mainstream religious practices that most people seeking a familiar alternative cannot make sense of it.

Thelema's teachings were uniquely suited to its time. The belief system, based on the idea that the human religion has gone through three phases or Aeons—each with a unique approach to the practice of spirituality—teaches that the first phase, the Aeon of Isis, took place during the ancient world, when female deities and a glorification of nature reigned supreme. Next the Aeon of Osiris, dominated by male gods and the motifs of sacrifice and rebirth. Finally, there is the Aeon of Horus, in which mankind currently dwells. Thelema characterizes this Aeon as one of individuality and self-realization, when individuals will take responsibility for their own spirituality.

Though Crowley started a Thelematic community in Italy, it was unsuccessful because of poor financing and Crowley's tendency to alienate potential recruits. The one society that bears his standard, Ordo Templi Orientis, actually predates Crowley's birth and though briefly led by Crowley, ousted him long before his death.

Despite Crowley's failings, Thelema and Ordo Templi Orientis have flourished since his death and inspired other cults and alternative beliefs including Scientology and Gardnerian Wicca, the basis of the modern wicca movement.

Variously loved and hated, the father of the modern occult movement was an iconoclast that left a long, if somewhat confusing, legacy. Crowley may be best characterized as someone who inspired other cults more than he did his own.

WORD AS BOND

HOLY TEXTS OF ALTERNATIVE BELIEF

Every major religion has its sacred text. Likewise, so do cults and alternative religious sects. Though some cult leaders prefer to keep their visions secret, many commit their theological systems to writing. Below are a few of the more well known.

- *Nag Hammadi Library* (found in Egypt in 1945) is a collection of texts exploring Gnosticism. Now woven into the fabric of most major religions, gnostic practice was seen as cultish in its own time.
- *The Book of Law* (Aleister Crowley's guide to Thelema) and its practices, while having all the language of a religion, is better understood as a set of self-help guidelines. Crowley used the text to advocate against evangelization and asked followers to lead by example.
- *Dianetics*, by L. Ron Hubbard is more of a collection of works than any one text. Hubbard traces a murky narrative describing the religion that begins with Dianetics, largely an alternative to psychiatry.
- *True Komix*, published by The Children Of God, was a series explaining the doctrine of the cult through anecdotes and vignettes. Each edition largely supported founder David Berg's notions involving sex as God's love.

Heaven's Gate leader Marshall Applewhite wrote several essays outlining himself as Jesus' reincarnation as well as a character in the Book of Revelations. Applewhite and Heaven's Gate co-founder Bonnie Nevins used these essays for recruitment purposes. Shoko Asahara of Aum Shinrikyo claimed that he was Christ reincarnated and tasked with taking on the sins of the world. His writings were less formal and he never codified a belief system.

IN THE NAME OF GOD

RELIGIOUS INTERPRETATION IN CULT FORMATION

Though cult leaders can lack genuine conviction, often acting out of a selfish desire to control, the ease of adapting religious language, rituals and beliefs makes religion the starting point of choice for the majority of cult initiants. The Peoples Temple, Heaven's Gate, Children Of God, and Aum Shinrikyo are just a few examples of cults that were inspired by Christian religious doctrine. Mormonism and Scientology also borrow heavily from religious history, symbolism, and language.

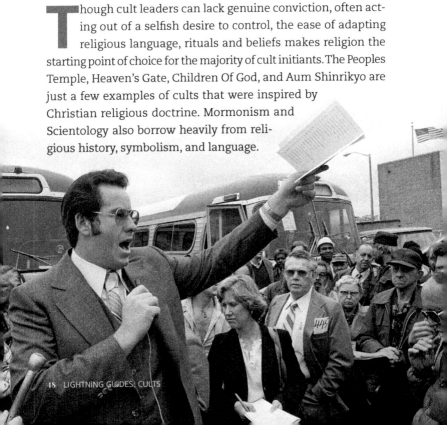

There are likely two reasons for the connections between cults and religions. First, creating a cult based on the teachings of an established religion makes it that much more accessible to those who might be attracted to it. For instance, there are 2.5 billion Christians in the world as of 2015. Building on their existing practice means gaining access to huge numbers of followers.

Second, splintering off large groups of followers from existing denominations by adjusting the doctrine makes the new doctrine appealing to followers, old and new. Many cult leaders were already members of established churches but were disillusioned with their leaders', teachings. Armed with righteousness and self-assurance, men like David Berg began preaching an alternative vision of the belief in which they already accepted as the truth. Evangelical Christianity is particularly susceptible to this because one of the core teachings is that individuals can communicate directly with God. Not surprisingly, there have been over a dozen figures in the last century claiming to be the resurrected Christ.

JESUS-COME-LATELY

Jim Jones, founder and spiritual leader of The Peoples Temple of the Disciples of Christ (Peoples Temple), described himself as an atheist or an agnostic throughout his life. An ardent believer in the power of individual will and collective work, when it came to devoting himself to a higher belief system, Jones chose Communism. Nevertheless, he was obsessed with religion as a

Left: Auctioneer Lloyd Ashman gestures as bidding gets high for three Peoples Temple buses in San Francisco, California (March 14, 1979). Assets of the cult went on auction by court order.

child, closely reading religious texts alongside the biographies of figures like Mahatma Gandhi, Joseph Stalin, and Adolph Hitler.

Jones had a sincere belief in the power of economic equality and social justice. Unfortunately, he was a liberal in a land of conservatives and spent most of his early days in Indiana being harassed for his Communist ideals. As the McCarthy witch hunt spread across the country, Jones began, cynically, considering joining the church as a way to share his beliefs. "How can I demonstrate my Marxism?" Jones says on an FBI tape recording, explaining his reasoning for joining the Methodist Church. "The thought was, infiltrate the church."

During his early years as a Methodist pastor in Indiana, Jones rarely spoke openly about his Communist beliefs, but they were evident in the causes he championed. Jones fought tirelessly for racial equality and his church was one of the first racially integrated congregations in Indiana. Jones also held massive evangelical revivals, where he would plant loyal members of his church amongst the crowd and stage fraudulent, rehearsed healing miracles. As distasteful as his means were, Jones' ends were hard to argue with—He spent most of the money raised at these revivals on housing, food, and education programs for Indianapolis' homeless population.

> *Nobody's gonna come out of the sky! There's no heaven up there! We'll have to make heaven down here!*

GREENER PASTURES

In the early 1960s, Jones moved his operation to northern California in search of a community more receptive to his beliefs. By the time he launched Peoples Temple in San Francisco, Jones had dropped all pretensions of a belief in God. Jones called his new doctrine "apostolic socialism," in which "those who remained drugged with the opiate of religion had to be brought to enlightenment—socialism."

The Peoples Temple quickly became a major force in San Francisco, both spiritually and politically, as Jones amassed over 5,000 members, though the Temple allegedly claimed a membership as high as 30,000. Jones attracted attention with his anti-religious sermons. "You're gonna help yourself, or you'll get no help! There's only one hope of glory; that's within you! Nobody's gonna come out of the sky! There's no heaven up there! We'll have to make heaven down here!" was a classic closer.

As the Temple grew, the responsibility of leading it became more complex and Jones couldn't keep his self-granted privileges a secret. Local newspapers started running features on the group, stories that would be the Temple's undoing. Former members reported sexual assault, child molestation,

MAIN MEN

Peoples Temple grew so politically powerful that members of the San Francisco government sought alliances with Jim Jones. These alliances included Harvey Milk, Jerry Brown, and even Willie Brown. Mayor George Moscone won a narrow victory with the help of Temple volunteers and appointed Jones as Chairman of the San Francisco Housing Authority Commission.

harassment, threats of physical violence, and portrayed Jones as an increasingly paranoid, drug addicted megalomaniac. Jones deflected these accusations as conspiracies created by the FBI, but by 1977 several former Temple members had created an oppositional group called Concerned Relatives and actively lobbied law enforcement agencies and politicians to investigate Jones.

Jones responded by moving members of the Temple to Guyana where he sought to create a perfect communist community. It was the final act of Peoples Temple as Jones began to exert more control over his followers and prosthelytized less about creating economic equality and social justice.

The Peoples Temple and Jim Jones began as most cults do, with a belief and desire to make the world a better place. During the course of the Temple's existence, Jones shepherded it through religious origins, to a politically-focused community, to a personal kingdom n Guyana. Finally, Jones had shed all vestiges of religion and transformed the Temple into a cult that ended in mass suicide and murder. The Peoples Temple was not the only cult to end in tragedy.

THE UFO CULT

Heaven's Gate, founded by Marshall Applewhite and Bonnie Nettles in the late 1970s, mixed Christology, eschatology, asceticism, and science fiction to create a religion-based belief system heavily featuring elements of science fiction. Applewhite and Nettles taught their followers that the Earth was "seeded" with human life by a race of extraterrestrials existing on a transcendent intellectual and spiritual plane, the Kingdom of Heaven. Two thousand years ago,

Right: Left behind in the Jonestown aftermath was this image of Rev. Jim Jones taken prior to his leading more than 900 members to their deaths.

PLANET EARTH [IS] ABOUT TO BE RECYCLED. YOUR ONLY CHANCE TO EVACUATE IS TO LEAVE WITH US.

—MARSHALL APPLEWHITE

these aliens decided that humans had evolved to the point where they might be able to comprehend alien intellect and higher truth. Jesus Christ was then chosen as the earthly vessel to be inhabited by a member of the Kingdom of Heaven so that he might guide enlightened humans. Applewhite claimed to observe the enlightenment process repeating itself—he professed his human form to be the new vessel of the Kingdom of Heaven. "I am in the same position to today's society as the one Jesus was in," Applewood claimed (in essays he distributed as recruiting material) The Earth and all life on it was about to be "ploughed under," as a farmer might do with a field of cover crops, Applewhite said. Only by following Applewhite on the path to join the aliens of the Kingdom of Heaven could one hope to avoid this imminent Armageddon.

Applewhite concluded that he and his followers needed to commit suicide as the comet Hale-Bop passed close to earth in March of 1997. According to Applewhite, Hale-Bop was a sign sent by the aliens to notify him of the world's demise. Once human souls were released from the earthly plane, Applegate believed they would be able to board a spacecraft sent by the aliens. Tragically, 38 followers believed Applegate's prophecy, followed his command, and took their own lives.

Where Jim Jones used religion as a cover for politics, Applewhite borrowed from religion, pop, and science fiction culture to promote his sensational beliefs and chimera. Although Jones and Applewhite were willing to follow their beliefs to death, not all cult leaders have been this committed to their professed ideals.

CARPET CLEANING CULT

Stewart Traill's Church of Bible Understanding (CBU) taught a version of evangelical Christian gospel mixed with a bohemian sensibility—members ate only natural foods and lived communally. By the time Traill started CBU—just nine years before, Traill was a self-employed carpet cleaner and outspoken atheist—he claimed *only he* could truly interpret the meaning behind God's word. Traill and his followers often wore pins with a boiled-down version of his pitch to potential recruits: Get Smart, Get Saved. This message apparently resonated, because just a few years after its founding in 1971, CBU had grown to almost 10,000 members, with 110 communes.

CBU members tithed (a practice in which followers donate a portion of their income to the church). With those tithes, Traill set

DID YOU KNOW

The 38 members of Heaven's Gate that took their lives were all wearing the same style of shoe, the Nike Decade. Saturday Night Live spoofed Nike with a fake ad that featured police photos of Heaven's Gate members' bodies wearing the shoes with the language, "Keds, worn by level-headed Christians everywhere." Applewhite chose the shoe because of its low price; they have never been reissued.

Seinfeld's Sunshine Carpet Cleaners is the name of a fictional carpet cleaning business (resembling Brothers Carpet Cleaning run by Church of Bible Understanding). The service doubled as a front used to brainwash people and recruit them into a religious cult.

up several businesses he staffed with his congregation—one of which was a vacuum cleaner repair company spoofed in a Seinfeld episode. Profits from the churches businesses flowed back to the church tax-free and Traill usually solely decided what to do with them. He built himself a massive mansion in Florida. When reports surfaced regarding the substandard conditions of the church's orphan homes in Haiti—homes Traill supposedly spent $2.5 million per year on—the IRS began investigating whether CBU even deserved tax exempt status.

The Church of Bible Understanding began unraveling when Traill could no longer hide the disparity between his opulent standard of living and the poverty level conditions in which his followers lived. By 2015 membership in the church had fallen drastically, though Traill still benefits from several profitable businesses the church owns.

Interpreting religious doctrine has been the jumping off point for many cults but not all leaders are as committed to their belief systems as others. Jim Jones used religion as a way to attract people to his radical political views and, in the end, was changed by his own approach, becoming the messiah he avowed against. Marshall Applewhite firmly believed in the religious basis of Heaven's Gate theology and, even though his preachings were laughably absurd, was as sincere as any mainstream religious leader. Stewart Traill appears largely to be an opportunist covering his materialist motives with religious wrapping. These men, like countless before and after, made strategic use of religious and cultural texts, bending both verse and ritual to support their intellectual, spiritual, and (in Traill's case) financial whim.

LEADING
LADIES

YOU KNOW MANSON, BUT WHAT ABOUT MADAME?

Nirmala Srivastava founded Sahaja Yoga in 1970 while at a meditation camp in Narjol, India. The camp was led by Rajneesh, a spiritual teacher focusing on dynamic meditation. During the camp, Nirmala experienced Primordial Kundalini and total spiritual awareness. Still, she believed Rajneesh to be a false spiritual guide and dedicated her life to opposing false gurus, instead preaching her own meditation practices.

Madame Blavatsky (Helena Blavatsky) co-founded the Theosophical Society in 1875 along with Colonel Henry Steel Olcott and William Quan Judge. Theosophy is a philosophy and belief focusing on understanding esoteric religions, pagan practices, and occult rituals. It seeks to understand hidden wisdom that can lead to personal spiritual enlightenment.

Clementine Barnabet In 1912 Barnabet, who was 18 years old, confessed to killing nearly 20 people as part of a religious group called the Church of Sacrifice. She believed that salvation was only achieved through human sacrifice, though her motives may have been materially oriented as well—many of her victims were robbed as well as murdered.

Silvia Meraz and her family worshipped La Santa Meurte, a Mexican female Saint of Death. Meraz and her son murdered two children and an adult male, dismembered their bodies and placed them on the saint's altar for sacrifice. Meraz believed ritual sacrifice would grant her wealth and protection from evil.

Mary Eddy founded Christian Science, a metaphysical branch of Christianity teaching that sickness and sin are illusions healed or removed by prayer. Furthermore, according to Eddy's faith, reality is purely spiritual and the material world itself is an illusion.

Aimee Semple McPherson (pictured above) an active evangelist in the early 1900s, was an infamously popular preacher of her day. She pioneered the use of media and spectacle in order to reach a wider audience and is credited as having influenced many of the television faith healers who followed in her wake. She founded Foursquare Church in 1923 and built its membership to nearly 8 million people.

PATH TO PROSELYTE

HOW JIM JONES BUILT HIS FLOCK

1

MULTI-MEDIA MARKETING PROGRAM
The Peoples Temple raises awareness with in-person proselytizing, pamphlets, direct mail and radio programs.

3

SERMONS
Curious people and new initiates attend a Jim Jones sermon in which he preaches a message of inclusiveness and human compassion.

2

RECRUITMENT DRIVES
involving hundreds of members and dozens of buses scour California for new recruits.

BECOME A CULT MEMBER

4

Recruits indicate their willingness to become Peoples Temple members.

6

ISOLATION
Connections outside of the commune are gradually eliminated. Members rely more and more on fellow believers for emotional, social, and even medical support.

7

SOCIAL SERVICES NETWORK
A large social services network helps members and non-members find work, clothing, food, and other basic necessities.

5

COMMUNES
New members work and live at Peoples Temple communes in Los Angeles, Redwood Valley, and San Francisco.

8

GOOD OF THE CHURCH
Members see the good done by Peoples Temple members and are fed a steady narrative of paranoid news about the outside world.

9

RAIDS & PARANOIA
Jones stages fake CIA raids to create an environment of perceived persecution.

10

STAY A CULT MEMBER

NOTORIOUS NOMADS

THE LONG ROAD TO INFAMY

S ome cults remain in fortified compounds, awaiting the end of days in privacy and security. Others prefer to move around, whether it be to avoid persecution, find greener pastures for recruitment, or seek spiritual enlightenment. Some of America's most notorious cults undertook long, arduous journeys before arriving at their final resting place—proving the boundless adaptability of cults and their members.

IN SEARCH OF HOLY GROUND

For Jim Jones and Peoples Temple, the first big move was both pragmatic and dogmatic. Jones had set up Peoples Temple in Indianapolis in 1955, and by the early 60s it had become fairly successful, attracting many members and slowly tightening its hold over their personal lives and possessions. As Jones' teaching drifted farther into Communism, however, he found it increasingly difficult to attract the stodgier Midwesterners of Indianapolis to

Left: 1978, Jonestown members, dead, after being forced to drink from a tub of grape Flavor Aid, poisoned with Valium, chloral hydrate, cyanide, and Phenergan.

his cause. In order to gain more followers, Jones decided a move was necessary. In 1961 Jones claimed to have seen a vision: thermonuclear war was imminent, and only those living in the right sections of the planet would be spared. Over the next few years Jones travelled around Brazil, exploring the idea of moving the cult there. In the end his efforts were unsuccessful and he returned to Indiana in 1963.

Two years later Jones told his congregation they must head west to California. There, Jones said, they would still be able to survive the nuclear war he foresaw coming as early as 1967. Jones and his most faithful followers packed up and relocated to Redwood Valley, California, a small town a few hours north of San Francisco. Jones initially found what he was looking for in Northern California. The remote locale would likely survive a nuclear war and was one of the few places in the US where a fiery preacher who equated capitalism with the Antichrist might find a receptive audience.

Jones and his congregation quickly outgrew Redwood Valley's recruiting opportunities and in 1970 he decided to move

{ **Apostolic Socialism** Jim Jones' term for his atheistic theology of Marxism, which promotes racial and socioeconomic equality. }

his congregation to San Francisco. It was in San Francisco that Peoples Temple would truely come into its own, developing a large and prosperous organization with strong ties to local businesses and politicians. Soon, Peoples Temple even began organizing state-wide recruiting expeditions after purchasing several Greyhound buses. They also established satellite churches in the cities of Los Angeles, Sacramento, and Fresno, among others.

JUNGLE KINGDOM

As the years wore on, Jones envisioned a utopia where he and his congregation could be free of capitalism corrosive culture. In 1974 he established a socialist paradise where Temple members could live in isolation and self-sufficiency in Guyana, naming it Jonestown. In early 1977 as few as 50 people lived in Jonestown; that changed, however, when Jones and the Temple received a large amount of negative media attention. The stories detailed Jones's megalomania and included testimonies from several for-mer members detailing sexual assault and physical intimidation. Jones left for Guyana in 1977 with nearly 900 people, Temple mem-bers and non, in tow. In November of that year, Congressman Leo Ryan arrived for his ill-fated inspection of the premises, setting off a chain of events that would lead to the Jonestown Massacre and the tragic end of the Peoples Temple.

Members who moved to Jonestown were forbidden to leave even though conditions were described as squalid. A congres-sional fact-finding mission, led by Congressman Leo Ryan, soon revealed that conditions were much worse than anyone had imagined. Ryan, initially set to travel to Guyana with only a few members of his staff, actually made the trip with a full entourage, including members of Concerned Relatives (a support group for Peoples Temple Family Members), a number of reporters, and a full team from NBC. Unfortunately, after meeting with several defectors, and Larry Layton (posing as a defector), Ryan was murdered at the Kaituma airstrip while trying to arrange the escape of several Jonestown families. The next morning, by the time the Guyanese army arrived at the Jonestown settlement, 909 of the members were found dead in what the Foreign Affairs Committee of 1979 called a "mass suicide/murder ritual."

DESERT PROPHET

Heaven's Gate travelled an equally long and winding path to eventual mass suicide. Its co-founders, Marshall Applewhite and Bonnie Nettles met in Houston in 1972, but accounts differ as to the circumstances. Some sources say they met in a hospital, where Nettles, a nurse, may have cared for Applewhite after a heart attack he suffered. Other sources say they met at a dance class. Whatever the circumstances behind their first encounter, Applewhite and Nettles soon discovered that they shared a deep and abiding interest in esoteric religious history and theology. The pair opened a bookstore together that quickly failed, after which Nettles divorced her husband so that she and Applewhite could embark on a journey of spiritual discovery.

For the next few years Applewhite and Nettles toured the southwest and the West Coast nearly non-stop in an attempt to recruit followers. By 1974 the pair was arrested in Texas for credit card fraud, and Applewhite was extradited to St. Louis, spending six months in jail for failure to return a rental car. In 1975 the two spent time in the new age enclave of Ojai, California, as well as Hollywood, Gold Beach, Redwood City, Arizona, Colorado and Oregon, where they expected (and waited for) a spaceship to land. It never did.

Frustrated by their lack of progress in building a church following, and confounded by the failed realization of their beliefs, in 1976 the pair announced they would no longer hold public meetings. For the next three years Marshall and Applewhite, along with a handful of followers, lived in campgrounds throughout Texas and the Rocky Mountains. In the late 70s one of the members received a large inheritance, allowing the group to rent houses, first in Denver, then in Dallas. The stability helped Applewhite and Nettles recruit followers and their flock grew to nearly 100 members.

FINAL REST

Nettles died in 1985, and afterwards Applewhite redoubled his commitment to further probing the depths of the cosmic mysteries they'd worked through together. The group kept a low profile until 1992, when it released a series of 12 recruitment tapes and also began to use the Internet for recruitment. In 1996 Heaven's Gate moved into a mansion in Rancho Santa Fe, California. Roughly a year-and-a-half later, the bodies of Applewhite and 38 other followers were found there, wearing matching outfits and armbands labeled "Heaven's Gate Away Team," a nod to the Star Trek series. And with that, at least as far Earthly locations are concerned, the cult's journey came to an end.

DESTINATIONS OF THE DEVOTED

FAMOUS CULT FOUNDINGS, LOCATIONS & DATES

1 SCIENTOLOGY CAMDEN, NJ, USA 1952
2 UNIFICATION CHURCH PUSAN, SOUTH KOREA 1954
3 BRANCH DAVIDIANS WACO, TX, USA 1955
4 PEOPLES TEMPLE INDIANAPOLIS, IN, USA 1955
5 MUJAHIDEEN-E-KHALQ TEHRAN, IRAN 1965
6 FAMILY INTERNATIONAL HUNTINGTON BEACH, CA, USA 1968
7 HEAVEN'S GATE HOUSTON, TX, USA EARLY 1970s
8 ORDER OF THE SOLAR TEMPLE GENEVA, SWITZERLAND 1984
9 AUM SHINRIKYO TOKYO, JAPAN 1984
10 MOVEMENT FOR THE RESTORATION OF THE TEN
COMMANDMENTS OF GOD RWASHAMAIRE, UGANDA LATE 1980s

THE SOURCE FAMILY

LOS ANGELES' QUINTESSENTIAL HIPPIE CULT

James Edward Baker, after returning from World War II as a decorated veteran, set out to create a new life for himself in the Eden of Los Angeles. Baker sought spiritual understanding through alternative beliefs including Kundalani Yoga, Vedanta, and other esoteric religious philosophies. Baker was also a stuntman. His machismo and chauvinism soon cultivated a proto-male reputation.

While in LA he fell in with a group of people that called themselves "The Nature Boys" and espoused a philosophy of living according to nature's laws; the laws consisted of a vegetarian diet and regular exercise. Baker, attuned to the times, opened several organic vegetarian restaurants in LA that attracted celebrities

including John Lennon and Marlon Brando. The businesses were a success and at the height of his wealth, Baker reported earning as much as $10,000 per day in the early 1970s.

Eventually, Baker changed his name to Father Yod, bought a mansion in the Hollywood Hills and started preaching a mélange of "mystery tradition." He invited mostly young, pretty women to live with him at his mansion and called the commune The Source Family, named after his first restaurant. Baker's wife, Robin, once commented, "You're just a dirty old man on a lust trip."

Father Yod attracted followers because of his money, the young women who followed him everywhere, and a psychedelic jam band he formed called YaHoWha 13. The band mostly improvised their compositions and, despite only a few of the members had much musical experience, the albums quickly become collectors objects.

In 1974 Father Yod sold his restaurants and moved the commune to Hawaii. In August of 1975, at 55 years old, Yod launched a hang glider off the top of a cliff on Oahu's eastern shore. Unfortunately, Yod had no experience piloting a glider and fell 1,300 feet to his death.

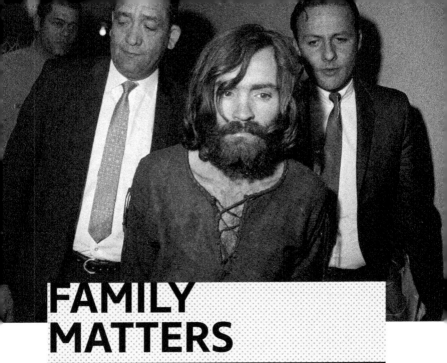

FAMILY MATTERS

A MANIFESTING OF CRIMINAL MINDS

No cult has left its mark so indelibly stamped onto the American psyche as the Manson Family and its leader, Charles Manson, born Charles Milles Maddox. Throughout his lifetime, Manson's bizarre blend of hippie aesthetic and psychopathic rage has catapulted him to the status of pop culture icon.

Above: Charles Manson being escorted to his arraignment on conspiracy-to murder charges in connection with the Sharon Tate murder case.

He remains the living personification of the macabre and violent tendencies that lurk within the human subconscious.

The Manson Family's story begins in 1967, during the fabled "Summer of Love," when nearly 100,000 hippies, dropouts, alternative intellectuals, artists, and political radicals converged on the Haight-Ashbury district of San Francisco in an attempt to join the countercultural experiment right at its source. Charles Manson was 33 years old and had spent the better part of his life in and out of prison. Many have attributed this to his childhood marked by poverty and extreme neglect.

Manson was homeless, panhandling, busking on the streets when he met librarian Mary Brunner in Berkley, California. Smitten with Manson's strange and intense charisma, Brunner agreed to let him move in with her. As with many of the Bay Area emigrés, Manson marketed himself as a spiritual prosthelityzer and attracted a small, mostly female audience receptive to his apocalyptic preaching. Brunner's home served as Manson's headquarters where he lived with as many as 18 women devoted to his beliefs and needs.

RAMBLING DOCTRINE

As a guru, Manson cobbled together elements of different alternative faiths that he had been introduced to in prison, particularly Scientology and the Process Church, an offshoot of Scientology. While his early teachings may have lacked originality and largely focused on an impending race war that would destroy the world, he made up for it with a dynamic and highly magnetic personality. This was on full display when the enraged father of one of Manson's female followers cornered him, pointed a shotgun at his head, and told him he was about to die. Destined for a different fate, Manson was able to calm the father down and persuade him to accept the life his daughter had chosen.

Day-to-day life in the Manson Family consisted mainly of sex with Manson, drugs with Manson, and music and proselytizing with Manson. Several of those initially attracted to him grew tired of his self-serving ways and left Manson's nascent cult. By the end of the Summer of Love, Manson and those who still prescribed to his preachings decided to leave San Francisco and travelled up and down the West Coast, finally settling in Los Angeles.

CELEBRITY CIRCLES

In 1968 Manson made the acquaintance of Beach Boys cofounder and drummer Brian Wilson. Wilson was so fond of Manson that he let the entire Family move into his LA mansion. Proximity to stardom attracted more followers and the Family grew from roughly a dozen to 24 members. All was not well in The Family,

OCCULT OBSESSIONS CULT PRACTICE IN POP CULTURE

1968

CHILDREN OF THE CORN Stephen King's supernatural horror film is set in fictitious Gatlin, Nebraska, where the children are enticed to ritually murder the adults for the sake of a rich corn harvest.

1981

TICKET TO HEAVEN

ROSEMARY'S BABY A psychological thriller in which a mother-to-be believes her husband is going to kill their baby in an occult ritual.

1984

TICKET TO HEAVEN In Ralph Thomas' feature length film, David, joins a cult that uses starvation, exhaustion, and brainwashing practices.

however. Wilson spent more than $100,000.00 for the medical treatment of various STDs that Manson and his followers spread amongst each other.

Accompanying Wilson on the LA celebrity party circuit, Manson met several music industry professionals and recorded extensively; those recordings wouldn't be released until after the murders Manson and The Family committed, making Manson a household name. During this time, no one suspected the horror that was to come. Al Lewis, an actor who let Manson babysit his children on several occasions, later stated that Manson seemed like "A nice guy when I knew him."

Wilson quickly grew tired of his new friends and kicked them out a few months after they arrived. The Family moved around between a few largely deserted ranches on the outskirts of LA. At one of these, the Spahn Ranch, Manson paid rent by forcing his followers to have sex with the establishment's 80-year-old owner. Around this time Manson was introduced to The Beatles and their *White Album*, which had just come out. Manson had long spoken to his followers about

SANTA SANGRE This Mexican-Italian horror chronicles the history of Fenix, a boy who spends his childhood with a cast of circus characters, including his mother, Concha, the leader of a religious cult.

THE DA VINCI CODE Directed by Ron Howard and starring Tom Hanks, this mystery portrays the Priory of Scion and Opus Dei as two cult-like organizations in search of the Holy Grail.

2001

1989

HARRY POTTER AND THE PHILOSOPHER'S STONE The most sinister of the four houses at Hogwarts, Slytherin's student body resembles a cult hierarchy.

2006

the racial tensions being stirred up by the Civil Rights Movement and his belief that it would ultimately lead to out-and-out conflict, but these views took on a more concrete form in late 1968.

Convinced the *White Album* was really about his group and his fantasies of an impending race war, Manson began studiously interpreting the album's lyrics and preached about Helter Skelter. Taken from the Beatles' song of the same name, Manson described Helter Skelter as an apocalyptic battle between blacks and whites. He formulated a plan involving releasing an album that would catalyze the conflict of Helter Skelter, during which he and The Family would hide out in a bunker. When the conflict ended, with the black population triumphant, Manson would emerge as their leader ushering in an era of racial harmony and peace.

CRIMINAL INTENT

Years of drug abuse irreparably altered Manson's already unhinged mind and his preaching and actions soon took on a violent bend. On

OCCULT OBSESSIONS CULT PRACTICE IN POP CULTURE

2011

THE MASTER Inspired by L. Ron Hubbard, founder of Scientology, this drama features an alcoholic sex addict who becomes attracted to a cult-like philosophical organization called "The Cause."

MARY MARCY MAY MARLENE Written and directed by Sean Dirkin, this film tells the story of a young woman, haunted by the memories of a painful past, and plagued by increasing paranoia. She flees an abusive cult to rejoin her family.

2012

July 1, 1969, Manson shot Bernard "Lotsapoppa" Crowe, a black drug dealer with whom he'd previously had a dispute. Three weeks later he instructed Robert Kenneth "Bobby" Beausoleil to murder Gary Hinman over a drug deal gone bad. After Beausoleil was arrested and charged with murder, Manson concluded he needed to act immediately before Helter Skelter slipped through his fingers.

On August 8, 1969, Manson instructed Charles Watson, Susan Atkins, Linda Kasabian, and Patricia Krenwinkel to break into Terry Melcher's house, whom Manson had met briefly through Dennis Wilson, and "totally destroy everyone in it, as gruesome as you can." Sharon Tate's presence at the house was a tragic coincidence considering that Melcher left for Italy the day before the murders and Tate was scheduled to leave the following day to join her husband Roman Polanski. The Family members carried out Manson's orders to the letter. Along with three friends who had been staying at the house, Tate and her unborn child were brutally stabbed to death. Messages like "pig," "rise," and "Helter Skelter," all veiled references to songs on the *White Album*, were scrawled on the walls in the victims' blood.

2014

TRUE DETECTIVE In this TV series, two police officers investigate a shadowy satanic cult tied to an evangelical movement.

2015

UNBREAKABLE KIMMY SCHMIDT

THE LEFTOVERS This post-rapture TV series features a couple in the fictional town of Mapleton, New York. The wife joins the Guilty Remnant, a cult for those "left behind."

2014

UNBREAKABLE KIMMY SCHIMDT The title character who was kidnapped and held hostage by a cult for 15 years, decides to move to New York to begin a new life.

The following night, Manson and Charles Watson, Patricia Krenwinkel, and Leslie Van Houten entered the home of super-market executive Leto LaBianca and murdered he and his wife, Rosemary, stabbing each of them dozens of times. Manson took the credit card from Rosemary's purse and left it in the bathroom of a service station located in a predominantly black area. The aim of both murders, apparently, had been to incite race riots in LA that would then sweep across the country.

Manson and nearly all of his fellow Family members were arrested after a protracted investigation by the Los Angeles Police Department. The subsequent trial proved problematic for the prosecution since several of Manson's followers testified that they were the sole perpetrators of the murders. Other Manson Family members held vigil outside the courthouse, which added to the media frenzy surrounding the case. It was only when Manson's legal defense team refused to call witnesses and closed their case that Manson was convicted. Many have since claimed that Manson was never given a fair trial and that his lawyers did only what they were legally required to do in order to ensure a conviction without the possibility of a retrial.

The Family was linked to several more murders and further arrests were made in the months following Manson's trial. Lynette Fromme, another Family Member, attempted to assassinate US President Gerald Ford in 1975 in retribution for Manson's incarceration. More than 30 years after his conviction, Manson still wows the media.

FLESH FIEND

VICTOR BARNARD LOVES YOUR CHILDREN

Victor Arden Barnard, 53, was arrested in Brazil in late February 2015 after nearly a year on the run. Barnard's cult, the River Road Fellowship, operated in a rural Minnesota town from 2000 to roughly 2012. Bernard convinced cult members to let their daughters—some as young as 12 or 13—stay with him at his compound, where they were repeatedly molested. The cult began to fall apart in 2009 when members learned Barnard had been having sex with their wives.

Barnard carried a staff and dressed in Biblical robes, referring to himself as "Christ in the flesh." In 2012 Barnard fled to Washington, and warrants were issued for his arrest in spring of 2014 over allegations of statutory rape. Most of the parents only learned at that time that Barnard had been abusing their daughters since 2000.

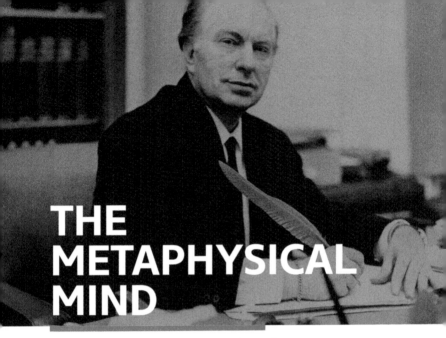

THE METAPHYSICAL MIND

SCIENTOLOGY SUES ITS WAY TO ACCEPTANCE

Originally envisioned as a self-help styled alternative to psychiatry, Scientology has evolved into a litigious, punitive cult. L. Ron Hubbard's belief system, first introduced to the world through his book *Dianetics* and subsequently codified in *Scientology, a Religious Philosophy*, has been dogged by controversy, lawsuits, deception, and tragedy from the moment of its introduction to the world.

Above: L. Ron Hubbard at his desk in April of 1999.

Scientology has all the components of a cult: a top-down leadership structure, violent coercion of members, secret theology that can only be revealed to those who join, reports of sexual abuse, and an aggressive, combative response to those that question its motives. Several countries have outright banned its practice—including France, Germany, and Australia—and for a brief moment L. Ron Hubbard was associated with a conspiracy to infiltrate the United States government in order to discredit it. Despite this, the IRS officially recognized Scientology as a religion by granting it tax-exempt status in 1993.

If nothing else, Scientology offers a fantastic tale of how a single individual has forced one of the most powerful governments in the world to acquiesce to his demands.

GRAND ILLUSIONS

In his youth, L. Ron Hubbard was a prolific pulp science fiction author looking to make more money than the dime store salary his profession provided him. Hubbard is remembered by several of his writing peers to have said that writing pulp was no way to make money and if a man wanted to become a millionaire he needed to start a religion. Good for his word, he published *Dianetics: The Modern Science of Mental Health* in 1950. Dianetics was a self-help system broadly inspired by concepts from 1930s pop psychology such as Ludwig Binswanger's treatise on existential therapy. Its main practice was auditing, a counseling technique intended to recall painful past memories and defuse their ability to influence a patient's current mental and emotional state by confronting them head on. *Dianetics* sold extremely well and Hubbard garnered many loyal followers over the next two years.

However, Hubbard's attempts to have his methods recognized by the medical community were unsuccessful as they were entirely based on subjective assumptions and anecdotal outcomes , unable to be recreated for peer review.

Though Hubbard had intended for *Dianetics* to be a psycho-therapeutic technique firmly grounded in science, the rejection by the medical world caused him to change tack—and formed his life-long rejection of psychiatry. In 1952 he published *Scientology, a Religious Philosophy* and shortly thereafter incorporated three churches of Scientology in New Jersey, a move critics call convenient timing given that his Dianetics organization had gone broke and lost its trademark to a creditor. Hubbard opened the first brick-and-mortar Church of Scientology in Los Angeles in 1954, and in 1957 the Church was granted tax-exempt status by the IRS; a move immediately reversed after they reviewed Hubbard's organization the following year.

ALIENS AND REPRESSION

Over the next decade, the Church attracted throngs of followers and Hubbard continuously wrote new material, constantly editing Scientology's theology. In 1967 Hubbard created the Sea Organization, a naval extension of the church. Publicly, Sea Org was described as the Church's research and development facility for its senior members. Privately, however, Hubbard found it easier to be a stateless person since the US government was limited in law enforcement once he left its territorial boundaries. He used the time onboard the ship to develop many of the concepts forbidden to all but the highest-level members of Scientology. This included his theory that Xenu, the alien dictator of The Galactic Confederacy, brought billions of his people to Earth 75 million years ago, then killed them in volcanos by dropping hydrogen bombs on them. The spirits of this mass murder are called Thetans and, according to Scientology, inhabit human bodies. Hubbard developed techniques to rid the body of these Thetans so that humans could become spiritually pure people. Hubbard's fully developed concept of Scientology has never been officially released by the church, but it is described in quasi-religious terms as, essentially, a complex self-help process known as The Bridge to Total Freedom.

Scientology requires a billion year commitment by its members.

The Bridge largely consists of an ongoing series of auditing sessions for which each member must be approved; each session costs a great deal of money to undertake. In these sessions, members investigate their pasts as well as events in past lives—Scientology requires a billion year commitment by its members—with the aid of an E-Meter, a device that measures electrodermal activity and that Scientologists believe can help ascertain the meaning of the events described in an auditing session. Scientologists also believe the human psyche is split into two parts: the reactive mind and the analytical mind. Through auditing, Scientologists attempt to realize the latent capabilities of the analytical mind. When this goal is finally realized, Scientologists refer to the resulting mental and emotional state as "clear" and deem the member spiritually realized.

The Scientology E-Meter and cans are shown along with books by L. Ron Hubbard, founder of Church of Scientology, at the church's community center in the neighborhood of South Los Angeles.

A VINDICTIVE SAVIOR

Basing your faith on a science fiction fantasy and charging your followers large amounts of money in order to be saved is a sure way to attract negative attention. Hubbard quickly found himself the target of press articles questioning Scientology's real intentions and a second IRS review of its tax-exempt status. In 1967 the IRS concluded that the Church was engaged in a number of commercial activities and operated for the personal benefit of Hubbard—Scientology's coveted tax-exempt status was subsequently revoked. The Church responded swiftly with a series of lawsuits that would last for the next quarter century, the longest-running legal dispute in IRS history.

Hubbard had anticipated public and government resistance and in the 1950s established the "Fair Game" policy, which states that any individuals or organizations that pose a threat to

Scientology—internally or externally—should be dealt with by any and all means necessary. This policy launched with Operation Snow White, a strategy targeted to undermine and reverse the IRS's ruling, and later grew into a major branch of the Church focused on PR and image control.

The operation entailed the infiltration of government agencies in over 17 countries, and ultimately became the single largest infiltration of the US government in history, with up to 5,000 Scientologist's involved. Through wiretapping, burglary and other covert means, Church members stole government documents, tracked personnel with intent to blackmail, and even attempted to plant false information in the IRS archives in order to later discredit the agency. The plot was uncovered and 11 high-ranking Scientologists, including Hubbard's wife, were found guilty of a number of serious charges against the government. Many served prison sentences as a result.

Methods of control within Scientology are every bit as brutal as attacks against outsiders. As members climb the ranks of the organization they become increasingly estranged from the outside world and the organization discourages the viewing or discussion of any outside materials that contradict its teachings. In 1965 the Church was banned in several Australian states, due to an investigation that found its practice of auditing amounted to a form of hypnotic brainwashing. Members who leave the Church, labeled "suppressive persons," are effectively cut off from members who remain, a policy that has broken apart the families of many.

THE LEGACY CONTINUES

There are widespread allegations of intense mental and physical abuse towards members that question the Church's teaching. David Miscavige, who became Scientology's leader after Hubbard's death

ALL CLEAR

Going Clear: Scientology and the Prison of Belief is an HBO documentary that details the history of the Church of Scientology and the brutal tactics it uses to keep its members in line. The film features several former members of the Church discussing the abuses they suffered as they began to doubt Scientology.

in 1986, sent dozens of the church's senior members to live in "The Hole," a squalid building housed on the premises of Gold Base, Scientology's California headquarters. Marty Rathbun and Mike Rinder, two of Scientology's most powerful members, were among those Miscavige set his sights on. Each reported disgusting conditions, beatings, verbal humiliation, and were coerced into confessing crimes they never committed. The former members sent to "The Hole" believe that Miscavige used Hubbard's death to consolidate his hold over the church. Since defecting, Rathbun and Rinder have been subjected to 24-hour-a-day harassment by Scientology's security arm.

Despite, or perhaps because of, all this, Scientology has prospered. Its wealthy members, many of them celebrities like Tom Cruise and John Travolta, give generously to the Church. The Church also has a number of different investments and owns real estate holdings valued in the hundreds of millions of dollars. In 1993 the IRS and the Church of Scientology reached an agreement to confer tax-exempt status once again. The terms of the agreement were never released but critics have framed it as a case of capitulation in the face of a sustained legal assault. As part of the agreement,

Scientology—which refused to recognize the 1967 decision and did not pay taxes for the entirety of its 25-year legal campaign—agreed to pay $12.5 million in back taxes, an amount suspected to be just a fraction of the total owed.

Scientology has survived federal investigation, public derision, and countless sealed lawsuits brought against it by former members, the press, and multiple governments from across the globe. Its endurance is a testament to the power of belief, however absurd, and the efforts of the cults' leadership to persevere in the face of a hostile environment. The controversy of its very existence points to the malleable nature of human spiritual understanding—where some believe it to be as authentic as Christ's resurrection, others see it as nothing more than a sophisticated and disingenuous bottle of snake oil.

FUELED BY FANTASY

DID WE ALL COME FROM ALIENS?

The Ancient Astronaut Theory is the belief that aliens visited Earth thousands of years ago and played a major part in the development of human culture. As you may expect, evidence is scant and instead adherents rely on conspiracy, interpretation, and closed systems of logic to promote their ideas. Though H.P. Lovecraft (1890–1937), the posthumously famous author of horror fiction including, "The Call of Cthulhu," *The Shadow Out of Time*, and *At the Mountains of Madness*, dismissed any attempts to endow his work with meaning beyond fantasy, many enthusiasts and tea-leaf readers have looked to his work as a sort of origination point for Ancient Astronaut Theory.

PROPHECIES OF A SECOND COMING

DAVID KORESH AND THE VOICE OF GOD

Had the FBI and ATF not raided the Branch Davidian compound in Waco, Texas in 1993, David Koresh and his followers would likely be seen as many cults are, a place to keep your children away from and an oddity to footnote in academic studies of religion. But because of the anti-government

Above: An altar placed at the Branch Davidians headquarters, Mount Carmel Center ranch in the community of Elk, Texas, nine miles east-northeast of Waco.

politics ushered in by President Ronald Reagan's administration, and carried forward by the Republican Party, Koresh and the followers that died with him have, in part, been turned into emblems of religious freedom and government intervention.

Koresh's beliefs were molded in religious tradition but they also represent a contemporary phenomenon in Christian society: an increasingly complex world often outpaces longstanding religious narratives. To account for this, religious leaders interpret doctrine to fit the issues of the day, resulting in belief systems that break with their traditional counterparts. Koresh was one such leader as his personal belief was the result of many different influences. He was steeped in Baptist tradition through the Davidians relationship with Seventh Day Adventism, but added to that was a messiah complex. Koresh believed himself to be Jesus reincarnated. He also experienced what many refer to Jerusalem Syndrome, when someone travels to Israel and receives visions or direct communication from God. Koresh's faith was a complex mix of tradition and progressive vision that ultimately served his own ego.

HUMBLE ORIGINS

David Koresh, born Vernon Wayne Howell in 1959, the son of a 14-year-old mother. Alternately cared for by his mother and grandmother, Koresh's early childhood was marked by loneliness and neglect. Koresh was a poor student and suffered from dyslexia, dropping out of high school in 11th grade. His only consolation while growing up was the Bible, which Koresh read voraciously. As early as the age of 12, he'd taken to lecturing other boys on scripture.

At the age of 22, Koresh joined the Seventh-Day Adventists and fell in love with the preacher's daughter but was expelled from the congregation when he asked the preacher to let him marry her. Shortly thereafter, he moved to Waco, Texas, to join the Branch Davidians.

At the time, 65-year-old Lois Roden was the spiritual leader of the Davidians. Lois took Koresh under her wing and he initially flourished as a devout follower. Koresh became a rising star in the isolated world of the Branch Davidians, and claimed to have received several visions while on a religious pilgrimage to Israel in 1983 with other members of the cult. Supposedly these visions unlocked the meaning of the Seven Seals in the Book of Revelations, a message Koresh called "The Serpent's Root."

Roden allowed Koresh to preach his message, a decision that didn't sit well with her son and heir apparent to the leadership of the Davidians, George Roden. When Lois died in 1985 tensions between George Roden and Howell grew. They finally came to a head when Roden and his loyalists forced Koresh and his followers to leave the compound at gunpoint. Koresh and his group moved to a hastily constructed

David Koresh, right, with his wife Rachel and son Cyrus. Date Unknown.

shanty-town 90 miles from Waco. They began an intensive recruitment drive during this period and travelled to Israel again, where Koresh claimed to have received another prophetic vision upon his return.

In 1987, Koresh attempted to claim leadership of the Davidian cult. Roden's hold on the compound was slipping, as many followers found him to be a paranoid, uninspired teacher. To prove his place at the head of the congregation, he challenged Koresh to see which of them could raise the dead. Roden exhumed a corpse and Koresh, strategically, called the police. The police asked for proof and Koresh and his followers returned to the compound, guns and cameras at the ready. A shootout ensued in which Roden was injured but Koresh was unable to provide the evidence required by the police. A testament to how little local law enforcement wanted

Smoking fire consumes the Branch Davidian Compound during the FBI assault, ending the 51-day standoff with cult leader David Koresh and his followers.

to get involved, during the ensuing trial Koresh stated that he shot Roden in an attempt to recover evidence of criminal activity and shouldn't be charged with a criminal act. The court agreed and he and his followers were released.

RETURN OF THE KING

Howell and his followers retreated to their encampment and waited. Later that year Roden, who had grown increasingly paranoid since the last incident with Koresh, killed Dale Adair with an axe after Adair claimed to be the true messiah. Roden was arrested, and Koresh (whose name was only officially changed in 1990 to reflect a combination of the Persian emperor Cyrus the Great—spelled Koresh in Persian—and King David) and his followers returned to unite the two groups under his leadership.

Befitting his position as a self-proclaimed prophet, Koresh soon began partaking in a host of sexually abusive activities. This involved taking his pick of the Davidian women, including girls as young as 13. Koresh stated, that according to God's will, he was destined to sire 12 children who would usher in an era of peace as rulers of the world. Surviving members reported that Koresh annulled the marriages of his congregation so he could take any woman he wanted as a "spiritual wife," meaning he could have sex with her. He also required celibacy from his male members, further concentrating his hold over the congregation.

The community lived peacefully for several years until 1993, when a local newspaper began publishing salacious articles outlining Koresh's sexual deviancy, including the molestation of young girls. The FBI and local law enforcement were never able to make the case for sexual abuse in part because, at the time, Texas allowed girls as young as 14 to marry and have sex with their parents' consent. Koresh's followers were quick to defend their prophet by making statements their children were married to other members with their consent and that Koresh only had one wife. The ATF persisted, however, after a UPS driver reported delivering automatic weapons and grenades to the Davidians.

DEATH OF A PROPHET

In February of 1993 the ATF served a warrant but were met with armed opposition—the Davidians had been tipped off to the raid by the remarkable coincidence of a television reporter asking directions of the compound from a postal worker who turned out to be Koresh's brother-in-law. A two-hour firefight ensued but soon ATF agents began to run out of ammunition. The Davidians had no such problems. After four ATF agents and five Branch Davidians had been killed, a ceasefire was called and the Davidians allowed the ATF agents to retreat.

After the failed raid, the FBI took over, encircling the compound and initiating a siege that would last 51 days, blasting loud music, flashing bright lights and using flash-bang grenades. Koresh was wounded during the initial raid, and in negotiations with the FBI said he couldn't surrender until he'd finished writing religious documents he was working on. On April 19 the FBI attacked, demolishing the compound's outer walls with tanks and firing smoke grenades. The main building that the Davidians had barricaded

Timothy McVeigh, architect of the April 19, 1995, Oklahoma City bombing that killed 168 people, carried out the terrorist act on the two year anniversary of the Branch Davidians standoff in Waco.

themselves inside caught fire, and within an hour nearly 80 Branch Davidians were burned alive. In the chaos, Koresh was shot in the head by his disgruntled second-in-command, Steve Schneider.

The FBI was criticized for its handling of the siege, including withholding baby formula after the cult had run out. Many argued that the FBI should have waited out the Davidians rather than using force. The siege and its aftermath were seen by many on the political right as an example of government overreach, lending Koresh and his followers the patina of martyrdom.

Were it not for their tragic ending, the Branch Davidians likely would have faded into obscurity, splintered into smaller groups over internal power struggles, or faced ongoing criminal investigations related to their sexual practices. Such is the fate of many cults similar to Koresh's. The siege and subsequent deaths of some 80 people have lent a mythos to the Davidians that live on to present times, ensuring the Koresh's legacy will live on.

WE'RE GOING IN

FEDERAL INVESTIGATIONS AND RAIDS

THE LORD OUR RIGHTEOUSNESS CHURCH
LEADER: WAYNE BRENT A.K.A. MICHAEL TRAVESSER
LOCATION: CLAYTON, NEW MEXICO
MEMBERSHIP: 80

Like the Branch Davidians, The Lord Our Righteousness Church was an offshoot of Seventh-day Adventism. Like many other self-styled prophets, Wayne had a taste for young girls, and at some point during the 2000s he allegedly began asking followers with young daughters to let him take them to bed. By 2008 word had gotten around to the authorities and Bent was arrested. That same year he was convicted of one count of criminal sexual contact with a minor and two counts of contributing to the delinquency of a minor and sentenced to 18 years in prison. He will be eligible for parole in 2016.

YEARNING FOR ZION RANCH
LEADERS: WARREN JEFFS AND DAVID S. ALLRED
LOCATION: ELDORADO, TEXAS
MEMBERSHIP: 700

The YFZ Ranch was a Fundamentalist Church of Jesus Christ of Latter-Day Saints community, one of many that broke with the mainstream Mormon Church when it decided to discontinue the practice of polygamy in exchange for more widespread

In this April 8, 2008 photo, law enforcement vehicles park on the grounds of the Yearning For Zion ranch, in Eldorado, Texas.

acceptance. In 2008 a local domestic violence shelter received a call from a 16-year-old girl who called herself Sarah, claiming that she was a member of the YFZ Ranch community and had been beaten and raped by older men.

Local police and Child Protective Services investigated, and ultimately arrested several men and removed almost all of the children in the community from their families, transferring them to an empty military facility. Some girls as young as 14 were found to be pregnant and investigators learned that pre-pubescent girls were married to men as old as 60. For the next three years, legal battles raged and the case garnered significant attention, with many arguing the authorities had gone too far in the wholesale separation of the community's families. In 2014 the state seized the YFZ Ranch. In a strange twist, the phone call from "Sarah" that started the whole ordeal was later found to be fake. The real "Sarah" was a serial crank caller, and had made several similar calls under different assumed identities in the past.

HERE AND NOW

CONTEMPORARY CULTS & NEW BELIEF

The Brethren, started in 1971 by Pentecostal minister Jimmie T. Roberts, believes the only way to prepare for the Second Coming is to abandon all worldly comforts. Accordingly, the group roams the US living in tents and scavenging most of their meals from dumpsters.

Eckankar was founded in Minnesota in 1965 and teaches its members that they can journey outside of their body and commune with God on the astral plane. Unsurprisingly, all proceeds from sales of the materials needed for the journey and commune go to the cult's leader.

The Kashi Ashram was founded in Florida in 1976 by Ma Jaya who claimed to receive visions from Jesus Christ and Hindu deities. Followers devoted themselves to practicing compassion and acted as caregivers to those afflicted with AIDS. Jaya sparked controversy when she asked her followers to give her their children for teaching.

New Mathura Vrindaban is an offshoot of Hare Krishna. This cult is based in the Northeast and Midwest of the United States. Members of the cult made millions of dollars for its founder Kirtanananda Swami through mail fraud, racketeering, and illegally selling copyrighted materials.

Raelism was founded in the 1970s by Claude Vorilhon. The cult promotes a liberal humanist philosophy centered around the belief that aliens created the human race. There is a heavy emphasis on sensual experience but Raelians treat sexuality as a matter of personal choice and responsibility.

Scientology claims to have 10 million active members. They do not back this up with any sort of hard evidence and Mike Rinder, a former high ranking member of the cult, pegs the number at no more than 30,000 people based on the church, direct mail membership list.

Unification Church was founded in 1954 by David Kim and Sun Myung Moon. Most recognizable by the name its adherents go by, "Moonies," this Christian-based faith has drawn criticism for many of its indoctrination techniques, including mass weddings and forced sexual rituals.

SIGNS OF THE TIMES

SOCIETY TURNS TO A NEW KIND OF LEADER

Almost every year, Apple Inc., unveils a new model of the iPhone. With each release, news organizations produce stories about customers—whom are variously described as devotees, Mac addicts, or members of the cult of Mac—lining up outside of retail stores, sometimes days in advance, so they can be some of the first consumers to hold their new product. This essentially buys and secures their membership in the Apple Kingdom. As of March, 2015, over 700 million iPhones have been sold.

The late founder of Apple, Steve Jobs (pictured above), has been variously described as a revolutionary, a visionary, and a megalomaniac who demanded perfection from his employees and publically humiliated those that challenged his vision. His cruelty towards those he disliked was only matched by his praise for those that satisfied his expectations. Andy Grignon, an iPhone engineer, said of being around Jobs, "You would always feel an inch tall." When Jobs died, Wall Street declared that no one could replace him as head of the company and the value of Apple fell by more than $100 billion in just over a year.

Apple is notorious for forcing its employees and subcontractors to work 60-, 70-, or 80-hour weeks; there are no guns being held to anyone's head but if you fail to meet expectations you will be replaced by someone else who will. Employees use words like "secretive," "intense," "stressful," "obsessive," "paranoid," and "insular" to describe the company's culture. They are forbidden from discussing their work at Apple with friends, family, and even other employees. Though the company's motto is, "Think different," it has rules, processes, and hierarchies described as the strictest of any company, ever. Still, those that work for Apple approve of the environment and even praise it.

In his biography of Jobs, Walter Issacson, noted that in many ways, Jobs built Apple in the image of himself; an image one might assume was influenced by the same Northern California environment that produced many of history's memorable cults and cult leaders. However, in place of salvation, Jobs promised his followers perfection. The vision he held for Apple and its products provided a personal value that was better suited for the times he lived in; shareholder.

Jobs is forgiven for his eccentricities because he built Apple into the most valuable company on the planet. He is emblematic of a new kind of prophet, one that society turns to as it loses faith in its religious institutions and political systems. Individuals no longer look to priests or presidents to show the way forward. The role of leader has been usurped by people like Jobs, people using their vision to build companies and sell products promising a new future - through innovation, they hold Armageddon at bay.

A PARTING THOUGHT

"Much of the attraction of the cult has to do with the grace of an early and romantic death. George Orwell once observed that if Napoleon Bonaparte had been cut down by a musket ball as he entered Moscow, he would have been remembered as the greatest general since Alexander."

—CHRISTOPHER HITCHENS

SOURCES

"A Believer Says Cult in Texas Is Peaceful, Despite Shootout". *New York Times*.
    March 6, 1993. Retrieved May 1, 2015.

"A Brief History of the Church of Scientology." A Brief History of the Church
    of Scientology. Accessed May 1, 2015.

"Accusations Against Sect in New Mexico." Associated Press report via
    the *New York Times*. May 4, 2008.

Anderson, Kevin Victor. "Report of the Board of Enquiry into Scientology."
    Victoria Board of Enquiry into Scientology. 1965. Melbourne: Government
    Printer. p. 155.

Applewhite, Marshall. "Do's Intro: Purpose—Belief." Do's Intro: Purpose—
    Belief. Heaven's Gate. Accessed April 24, 2015.

Atkins, Susan, and Bob Slosser. "Child of Satan, Child of God." Plainfield, NJ.
    Logos International. 1977. Print.

Barclay, Shelly. "Top 5 Cults Still Around Today." Historic Mysteries.
    December 2, 2013.

Barker, Eileen. "Watching for Violence." CESNUR, 2001. April 29, 2015.

Bearak, Barry. "Eyes on Glory: Pied Pipers of Heaven's Gate." The *New York
    Times*. Retrieved May 02, 2015.

Behar, Richard. "Scientology: The Thriving Cult of Greed and Power." *Time*.
    Archived from the original on August 19, 2013. Retrieved May 1, 2015.

Bell, Bill. "The Church of Bible Understanding; Minister Accuses Church
    of Enticing Youngsters." The Evening Independent. June 11, 1983.
    Accessed February 6, 2010.

Berry-Dee, Christopher. The Voices of Serial Killers the World's Most Mania-
    cal Murderers in Their Own Words. New York: Ulysses, 2011. Print.

Beyer, Catherine. "Who Is Overlord Xenu?—Scientology's Creation Myth."
    Alternative Religions. About.com. Accessed April 23, 2015.

Bogdan, Henrik, and Martin P. Starr. Aleister Crowley and Western Esoteri-
    cism. New York: Oxford UP, 2012. Print.

Bogdan, Henrik; Starr, Martin P. (2012). "Introduction." In Bogdan, Henrik;
    Starr, Martin P. Aleister Crowley and Western Esotericism. Oxford and
    New York: Oxford University Press. pp. 3–14.

Booth, Martin (2000). A Magick Life: The Biography of Aleister Crowley.
    London: Coronet Books.

"Bonnie Lu Nettles Biography." A&E Networks Television. Accessed
    May 2, 2015. Bio.com.

"Brazil Arrests U.S. Cult Leader Victor Arden Barnard, Wanted on Child Sex
    Charges." NBC News. Associated Press. February 28, 2015.

Bromley, David G. Cowan, Douglas E. "The Church of Scientology." In
     Gallagher, Eugene V. Ashcraft, W. Michael. 2006. Introduction to New and
     Alternative Religions in America 5. Westport CT: Greenwood Press.

Bugliosi, Vincent, and Curt Gentry. Helter Skelter: The True Story of the
     Manson Murders. New York: Norton, 1974. Print.

Burnett, John. "Two Decades Later, Some Branch Davidians Still Believe." NPR.
     NPR, 20 Apr. 2013. Web. 01 May 2015.

Bury, John Bagnell, "History of the Later Roman Empire from the Death of
     Theodosius I. to the Death of Justinian", The Suppression of Paganism,
     ch22, p. 371, Courier Dover Publications, 1958.

"Charles Manson—Internet Accuracy Project." Internet Accuracy Project.
     Internet Accuracy Project. January 1, 2012.

Church of Scientology charged in member's death. http://www.sptimes.com
     /TampaBay/111398/scientology1115.html

Colavito, Jason. "The Cult of Alien Gods: H.P. Lovecraft and Extraterrestrial
     Pop Culture." Amherst, NY: Prometheus, 2005. Print.

Cox, Savannah. "Five Utterly Insane Cults Still Active Today." All That Is
     Interesting. November 7, 2012.

Crowley, Aleister. The Book of the Law: Liber Al Vel Legis: With a Facsimile
     of the Manuscript Received. April 8, 9, 10, 1904. York Beach, ME. Weiser.
     2004. Print.

"Cults & Mind Control." Langone, Michael, Ph.D. "Cults and Mind Control."
     International Cultic Studies Association. Accessed April 20, 2015.

"CULTWATCH." CULTWATCH | One of the Web's First Cult Information Sites.
     Accessed April 29, 2015.

Emmons, Nuel. "Manson in His Own Words." Grove Press, New York. 1988.

"FAQ on 'Start a Religion'" Non-scientologist Faq on "Start a Religion" Bible.
     Accessed April 25, 2015.

Farley, Robert. "Scientologists settle death suit." May 29, 2004.
     St. Petersburg Times.

Fisher, Ian. "Uganda Cult's Mystique Finally Turned Deadly." April 1, 2000.
     New York Times.

Fantz, Ashley. "Who Was David Koresh?" CNN Cable News Network.
     April 14, 2011.

Frantz, Douglas. "Scientology's Puzzling Journey From Tax Rebel to Tax
     Exempt." New York Times. March 9, 1977. Archived from the original on
     March 21, 2008. Accessed May 1, 2015.

Furnham, Adrian. "Why Do People Join Cults?" February 24, 2014. Psychology Today. Accessed April 20, 2015.

"Going Clear: Scientology and the Prison of Belief." Dir. Alex Gibney. HBO Online. 2015.

Guinn, Jeff. Manson: The Life and Times of Charles Manson. New York: Simon and Schuster, 2014. Print.

Guinn, Jeff. "The Life and times of Charles Manson." London: Simon & Schuster, 2013. Print.

Hall, John R. Gone from the Promised Land: Jonestown in American Cultural History. 1987. New Brunswick, New Jersey: Transaction Publishers.

"Heaven's Gate: A Timeline | The San Diego Union-Tribune." Heaven's Gate: A Timeline | The San Diego Union-Tribune. BBC. March 18, 2007.

Helena; Tau Apiryon. "The Invisible Basilica: The Creed of the Gnostic Catholic Church: An Examination." Retrieved 29 Apr 2015.

Hubbard, L. Ron. Dianetics. Los Angeles, CA: American St. Hill Organization, 1950. Print.

Introspection Rundown http://www.xenu-directory.net/practices /introspection1.html

Johnson, Alex. "Cult Leader Victor Arden Barnard Charged With Child Sex Abuse." NBC News. NBC News, 16 Apr. 2014. Web. 25 Apr. 2015.

Jones, Jim. "The Letter Killeth." Original material reprint. Department of Religious Studies. San Diego State.

Jones, Jim. "Transcript of Recovered FBI tape Q 134." Alternative Considerations of Jonestown and Peoples Temple. Jonestown Project: San Diego State University.

Jonestown: The Life and Death of Peoples Temple. Dir. Stanley Nelson. PBS, 2007. Online.

Karoglou, Kiki. "Heilbrunn Timeline of Art History." Mystery Cults in the Greek and Roman World. Metropolitan Museum of Art. Accessed April 21, 2015.

Kimura, Rei. Aum Shinrikyo: Japan's Unholy Sect. North Charleston, SC: GreatUNpublished, 2002. Print.

Kopimism: the world's newest religion explained. http://www.newscientist .com/article/dn21334-kopimism-the-worlds-newest-religion-explained .html#.VZR2gedLsV8

Kreitner, Richard. "February 28, 1993: The Feds Raid the Branch Davidian Complex in Waco, Initiating a Long Siege." The Nation. Accessed May 2015.

Lalich, Janja. "Sexual Exploitation of Women In Cults." RELIGIONS CELL. Cultic Studies Journal. March 19, 2013.

"Largest Religious Bodies." Adherents.com. Accessed May 1, 2015.

Larson, Bob. 2004. Larson's Book of World Religions and Alternative Spirituality. Tyndale House Publishers, Inc.

Layton, Deborah. "Seductive Poison a Jonestown Survivor's Story of Life and Death in the Peoples Temple." New York. Anchor. 1999. Pg. 53. Print.

Lewan, Todd. "Polygamists transformed rocky ranch into bustling site." April 19, 2008. *Houston Chronicle.*

"List of officially recognized religions in Poland." February 25, 2013.

Malko, George. Scientology: The Now Religion. pp. 58. Delacorte Press, 1970.

Mathison, Richard. "Faiths, Cults & Sects of America: From Atheism to Zen." New York. Bobbs-Merrill. 1960. Print.

"What is the Sea Organization?" Church of Scientology. p. 26–27. Accessed May 1, 2014.

Melton, J. Gordon. "The Church of Scientology." 2000. Salt Lake City. Signature Press.

Miller, Russell. "Barefaced Messiah, The True Story of L. Ron Hubbard." First American Edition. 1987. New York. Henry Holt & Co.

Miller, Russell. (15 November 1987). "Farce and fear in Scientology's private navy [extract from "Bare-Faced Messiah: The True Story of L. Ron Hubbard"]" (PDF). *The Sunday Times.* Retrieved 1 May 2015.

"Mystery of the Vanished Ruler." *Time.* Accessed May 1, 2015.

Narcissistic personality disorder—*Diagnostic and Statistical Manual of Mental Disorders.* 4th ed. Text Revision (DSM-IV-TR) American Psychiatric Association.

National Assembly of France report No. 2468

"New Mexico Apocalyptic Sect Leader Gets 10 Years in Sex Case." AP (Las Vegas, N.M: Fox News). 31 Dec 2008. Retrieved 2 Mar 2010.

Newport, Kenneth G. C. *The Branch Davidians of Waco: The History and Beliefs of an Apocalyptic Sect:* Oxford, Oxford University Press, 2006).

Niebuhr, Gustav. "'The Family' and Final Harvest." *Washington Post.* The Washington Post, 2 June 1993. Web. 27 Apr 2015.

Nestel, M.L. "Inside the Sex Cult of 'Christ'." The Daily Beast. *Newsweek* /Daily Beast, 5 Feb 2015. Web. 25 Apr 2015.

Newport, Kenneth G. C. The Branch Davidians of Waco: The History and Beliefs of an Apocalyptic Sect: Oxford, Oxford University Press. 2006.

Orpheus, Rodney. Abrahadabra. Weiser, 2005.

Ortega, Tony (September 27, 2001). "Sympathy For The Devil: Tory Bezazian was a veteran Scientologist who loved going after church critics. Until she met the darkest detractor of all." New Times Los Angeles.

Partridge, Christopher H. UFO Religions. London: Routledge, 2003. Print.

Pick-Jones, Antoinette. "Jim Jones and the History of Peoples Temple." Alternative Considerations of Jonestown Peoples Temple. San Diego State University, 2007. Web. 24 Apr 2015.

Pitts, William L. "Davidians and Branch Davidians" Handbook of Texas— Texas State Historical Association. Retrieved 25 Nov 2012.

Piven, Jerry S. (2002). Jihad and Sacred Vengeance: Psychological Undercurrents of History. iUniverse. pp. 104–114.

Queen, Edward L.; et al. (2009). 'Seventh-day Adventist Church' in Encyclopedia of American religious history, Volume 3, 3rd ed. New York, NY: Infobase Publishing. p. 913.

Ramsland, Katherine. "The Story of Robin Gecht and the Notorious Chicago Rippers." Crime Library. truTV.com/Turner Broadcasting. Retrieved 28 Apr 2015.

Rawles, Neil. (February 2, 2007). Inside Waco (Television documentary). Channel 4/HBO.

Reiterman, Tim and John Jacobs. Raven: The Untold Story of Rev. Jim Jones and His People. Dutton, 1982.

Rhoads, Kelton, Ph.D. "Cult Influence & Persuasion Tactics." Cult Influence & Persuasion Tactics. Working Psychology, 5 June 1997. Web. 20 Apr 2015.

Rich, Nathaniel. "The Man Who Saves You from Yourself." Harpers Magazine. Harpers Magazine, 5 Nov 2013. Web. 20 Apr 2015.

"Roommate stunned by claims Colo. woman's bogus call triggered FLDS raid." Salt Lake Tribune. 20 Apr 2008

Sabotage, Sara. "Top 10 Crowley Myths Which Are Actually True." Aleister Crowley 2012. Aleister Crowley 2012, 04 Aug 2012. Web. 29 Apr 2015.

"Scientology May Be Demonized around the World, but in Israel It Barely Makes Waves—National." Haaretz.com. Associated Press, 8 Nov 2012. Web. 30 Apr 2015.

"Sexual Assault Response Consultative Team." Sexual Assault Response Consultative Team. George Washington University, n.d. Web. 27 Apr 2015.

Shipley, Graham (1999). "Chapter 5—Religion and Philosophy," The Greek world after Alexander, 323–30 B.C., Routledge.

Shklovski, I.S and Carl Sagan. Intelligent Life in the Universe. San Francisco: Holden-Day, 1966

Singer, Margaret. "Cults in Our Midst." Wiley. Revised edition, 2003.

Sutin, Lawrence. Do What Thou Wilt: A Life of Aleister Crowley. New York: St. Martin's Griffin, 2002. Print.

"Texas concedes sect woman who gave birth is adult." WOAI-TV. 15 May 2008.

"Texas Seizes Polygamist Warren Jeffs' Ranch." NBC News. Associated Press. 17 Apr 2014. Retrieved 18 Apr 2014.

"The Church of Bible Understanding; Minister Accuses Church of Enticing Youngsters." The Evening Independent. 11 Jun 1983. Retrieved 6 Feb 2010.

TheHuffingtonPost.com, 29 Sept 2013. Web. 21 Apr 2015.

The United Press (13 April 1934)."Confessed Genius Loses Weird Suit." The Pittsburgh Press. Retrieved 29 Apr 2015.

Tobias, Madeleine Landau, and Janja Lalich. "Psychopathy and the Characteristics of a Cult Leader." Captive Hearts, Captive Minds: Freedom and Recovery from Cults and Abusive Relationships. Alameda, CA: Hunter House, 1994. 67–79. Print.

Tobin, Thomas C; Childs, Joe (January 13, 2013). "Scientology defectors describe violence, humiliation in "the Hole"." *Tampa Bay Times*.

"True Komix." XFamily. N.p., n.d. Web. 29 Apr 2015.

True Komix #293 DO "The Little Flirty Fishy" The Family International. Web. 28 Apr 2015.

Two Years After Steve Jobs' Death, Is Apple a Different Company? http://business.time.com/2013/10/04/two-years-after-steve-jobs -death-is-apple-a-different-company/

Urban, Hugh B. (June 2006). "Fair Game: Secrecy, Security, and the Church of Scientology in Cold War America." Journal of the American Academy of Religion (Oxford University Press) 74 (2): 356–389.

Valentine, Carol A. (2001). David Koresh and The Cuckoo's Egg—pt. 3.

Marc Breault and Martin King, Inside the Cult, Signet, 1st Printing June 1993.

Various. "When Does a Cult Become a Religion?" Ethical Conundrums. The Guardian. 21 Apr 2015.

Victor, Jeffrey S. Satanic Panic: The Creation of a Contemporary Legend. Chicago: Open Court, 1993. Print.

Vogelstein, Fred. "And Then Steve Said, 'Let There Be an iPhone.'" 4 Oct 2013. http://www.nytimes.com/2013/10/06/magazine/and-then -steve-said-let-there-be-an-iphone.html?pagewanted=all&_r=1

Wallis, Lynne. "Born into a Sex Cult: Natacha Tormey on How She Survived Those Dark Days, Escaped, and Finally Built a New Life." *The Independent*. Independent Digital News and Media, 11 Aug 2014. Web. 22 Apr 2015.

Wasson, R. Gordon, Albert Hofmann, and Carl A. P. Ruck. "Kykeon Chemistry." The Road to Eleusis: Unveiling the Secret of the Mysteries. New York: Harcourt, Brace, Jovanovich, 1978. 151–57. Print.

Watkins, Paul, and Guillermo Soledad. My Life with Charles Manson. New York: Bantam, 1979. Print.

Wessinger, Catherine. How the Millennium Comes Violently: From Jonestown to Heaven's Gate. Seven Bridges Press, 2000.

"What Apple Employees Say About The Company's Internal Corporate Culture." http://www.businessinsider.com/what-apple-employees -say-about-the-companys-internal-corporate-culture-2013 -10#justin-maxwell-user-interface-designer-first-rule-of-apple -dont-talk-about-apple-1

Willey, Peter. Eagle's Nest: Ismaili Castles in Iran and Syria. London: I.B. Tauris, 2005. Print.

Wilson, Bryan (1970). Religious Sects: A Sociological Study, McGraw-Hill.

Wilson, Colin (2000). The Devil's Party, London: Virgin Books.

Wright, Stuart A. (ed.). Armageddon in Waco: Critical Perspectives on the Branch Davidian Conflict (Chicago: University of Chicago Press, 1995).

Wray, Daniel D. "This Is How Cults Work." VICE. VICE, 16 Dec 2014. Web. 20 Apr 2015.

Zeller, Benjamin E. Heaven's Gate: America's UFO Religion. Print.

Zeller, Benjamin E. "Scaling Heaven's Gate: Individualism and Salvation in a New Religious Movement." 2006. Nova Religio. University of California Press. 75–102.

INDEX

mental breakdowns, 32
Meraz, Silvia, 59
mescaline, 34
messiah, 16, 57, 91, 94
Middle East, 92
Milk, Harvey, 51
Miller, William, 39
Millerism, 39
Miscavige, 85
Modern cults, 40
molestation, 33, 51, 95
money, 10, 15, 27, 50, 71, 81–84
Moon, Sun Myung, 21, 101
Moonies, 101
Mormon Church, 21, 98
Mormonism, 10, 48
murder ritual, 66
murder, 52, 72, 75
murders, 13, 77–78
mysteries, 22
mystic traditions, 41

N

Nag Hammadi Library, 47
NPD (Narcissistic Personality
    Disorder), 14, 18
narcotics, 36
Native American, 34
Nature Boys, 70
Nettles recruit followers, 67
Nettles, Bonnie, 52, 66–67
Nevins, Bonnie, 47
New Mathura Vrindaban, 101
nicotine, 36
Nirmala Srivastavafounded Sahaja
    Yoga, 58

O

Oklahoma City bombing, 96
Olcott, Colonel Henry Steel, 58
Operation Snow White, 85
Ordo Templi Orientis, 45
orthodoxy, 11

P

pagan practices, 58
pair, 66, 67
paranoid, 52, 93, 94, 103
participants, 19
path, 54, 60–61, 66
Peoples Temple, 10, 13, 26, 31, 48–49,
    51–52, 63, 65
Peoples Temple Family Members, 66
periodicals recruiting members,
    independent, 31
Persephone, 23
personality traits, 14
peyote, 34
philosophy, religious, 34, 70, 80, 82
police, 93–94
political philosophy, 18
praise, 102–103
Primordial Kundalini, 58
prison, 73, 85, 98
Prison of Belief, 86
prophecies, 90–93
prophet, 66, 95–96, 103
Proselyte, 60–61
prostitutes, 34
Prostitution, 32
Protestantism, 39
PSI Mind Development Institution, 26
psychiatry, 32, 47, 80, 82
psychology, 37, 81

training, 22
traits, of cult leaders, 13–15
Travesser, Michael, 98
True Komix, 47

U

Underhill, Evelyn, 42
Understanding cult leaders, 13
Unification Church, 21, 101
United Nuwaubian Nation of
    Moors, 33

V

Van Houten, Leslie 78
Vedanta, 70
Vietnam War, 18
violent coercion, 81
visions, 47, 91, 92, 100
Vorilhon, Claude, 101

W

Watson, Charles, 77
White Album, 75–77
White, Ellen G., 39
Wilson, Brian, 74–75
Wilson, Dennis, 77
Worship, 22–23

Y

YaHoWha, 71
YFZ Ranch, 98–99
York, Dwight, 33
Youth, 36

Z

Zion Ranch, 98

CONTINUE THE
CONVERSATION

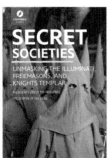
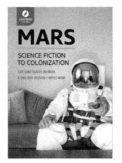